ORDER WIT

ORDER WITHOUT POWER

An Introduction to Anarchism,
History and Current Challenges

Normand Baillargeon
Translated by Mary Foster

Seven Stories Press
New York

Originally published in French as *L'ordre moins le pouvoir: Histoire & actualité de l'anarchisme*

English translation ©2013 by Mary Foster

Seven Stories Press
140 Watts Street
New York, NY 10013
www.sevenstories.com

Book design by Jon Gilbert

College professors and high school and middle school teachers may order free examination copies of Seven Stories Press titles. To order, visit www.sevenstories.com/textbook or send a fax on school letterhead to (212) 226-1411.

Library of Congress Cataloging-in-Publication Data

Baillargeon, Normand, 1958-
  [Ordre moins le pouvoir. English]
  Order without power : an introduction to anarchism, history and current challenges / Normand Baillargeon ; translated by Mary Foster. -- A Seven Stories Press first edition.
      pages cm
  Translation of the author's L'ordre moins le pouvoir.
  ISBN 978-1-60980-471-8
  1. Anarchism. 2. Anarchists. I. Title.
  HX833.B25413 2013
  335'.83--dc23
                                    2013008719

Printed in the USA.

9 8 7 6 5 4 3 2 1

CONTENTS

To be governed is to be kept in view, inspected, spied upon, directed, subjected to legislation, regulated, penned in, indoctrinated, preached to, controlled, weighed up, estimated, censured, commanded. It is, at each turn, each transaction, each move, to be noted, registered, added to the census, tariffed, stamped, measured, marked, subscribed, patented, licensed, authorized, authenticated, admonished, impeded, reformed, redressed, corrected. It is, in the name of public utility and the general interest, to be harnessed, exercised, blackmailed, pressured, monopolized, concussed, mystified, stolen.

—Pierre-Joseph Proudhon

Power is crap. That's why I am anarchist.

—Louise Michel

I am a partisan of social and economic equality, because I know that without this, equality, liberty, justice, human dignity, morality and the well-being of individuals as well as the prosperity of nations are only lies. But because I am at the same time a partisan of freedom, the first condition of humanity, I believe that equality should be established in the world by a spontaneous organization of labor and of collective ownership, by the free federation of communes, but certainly not by the supreme and tutelary action of the state. As long as economic and social equality do not exist, political equality will be a lie.

—Mikhail Bakunin

No God no master. Better to be.

—Jacques Prévert

*Anarchism is a tendency in the history of human thought
and action which seeks to identify coercive, authoritarian,
and hierarchic structures of all kinds and to challenge their
legitimacy—and if they cannot justify their legitimacy, which
is quite commonly the case, to work to undermine them and
expand the scope of freedom.*

—Noam Chomsky

INTRODUCTION

Declare yourself to be an anarchist and you are—almost inevitably—taken for a nihilist, a cheerleader of chaos, or even a terrorist.

Nothing could be further from the truth. This is a distortion resulting from decades of skillfully cultivated confusion around the concept of anarchism. Dictionaries are no exception; they generally foster the same preconceptions and prejudices. According to *Le Robert*, anarchism is supposed to be "Absence of government; confusion or disorder which results."

"Absence [*an*] of government [*archie*] and thus disorder and chaos," declares *Le Littré*. *Larousse* concludes that "the anarchist doctrine presents a peculiar mixture of disinterested illuminism and blind or brutal violence." One wouldn't know how to do any worse in so few words.

Elite culture, such as that encountered in academia, sometimes scarcely does better. For example, the relativist and irrationalist epistemology of Paul Feyerabend was recently described and discussed as an anarchist theory of knowledge. This indicates a complete ignorance of anarchism, and of the rationalism that has always inspired it.*

What is anarchism, if all of this is far from the mark?

Etymologically, anarchism is defined as [an-] (privative) [archos] (power, commandment, or authority). Taken literally, it is thus the absence of power or authority. This does not mean confusion or disorder if we accept that the order imposed by authority is not the only possible kind of order. Expressed as simply as possible, this is indeed what anarchism contends. Anarchists believe that this order in the absence of power will be born of freedom—freedom being the mother of order and not its daughter, as Pierre-Joseph Proudhon asserted. In other words, anarchism believes that, in the end, disorder may well only be "order without power," in the fine words of Léo Ferré.

Anarchists have incessantly highlighted the antiauthoritarian aspect of their philosophy. For example, Sébastien Faure wrote, "Those who refuse authority and fight it are anarchist." Similarly, Proudhon stated, "No more authority: not in church, state, land, or money." It would be easy to find many more such statements. I once met an old woman who had fought in the Spanish Civil War. She put it very simply, "I am an anarchist: that is, I don't like to give or receive orders."

As can be imagined, to the authorities this idea is unforgiveable; it is an unacceptable ideal. It is thus neither forgiven nor accepted.

---

* In the famous book, *Against Method* (1975), the Austrian philosopher Paul Feyerabend (1924–1994) argued that there are no methods or rules for seeking the truth in the sciences: "Anything goes." He concluded that science is just one means among others of acquiring knowledge, equivalent to religion or any other tradition, like astrology.

As a first approximation, then, we can say that anarchism is a political theory in which the idea of anti-authoritarianism is central. That is, it is a conscious and rational rejection of all illegitimate forms of authority and power. Of course the question then becomes: What constitutes illegitimate power? There are unquestionably powers and forms of authority that pass the test of legitimacy and to which anarchists are willing to submit. As Georges Brassens put it, "I am such an anarchist that I go out of my way to cross at the crosswalk!"

What are these legitimate powers and forms of authority? Why are they legitimate? There are no simple or definitive answers to these questions. All the less so because anarchism maintains that with the advance of freedom, the field of legitimacy can be revisited and legitimacy denied to forms of power previously accepted as justifiable.

Drawing out the theoretical and practical implications of this antiauthoritarianism, anarchism is the passionate love of freedom and equality. It gives birth to the profound conviction—or I should say hope—that relations freely consented to are best suited to our nature; that they alone are definitively capable of ensuring the harmonious organization of society. In the final analysis, they thus constitute the most adequate means of satisfying what Peter Kropotkin called the "infinite variety of needs and aspirations of a civilized being."

Anarchism sometimes asserts these ideas in turbulent contexts of revolt. This revolt, aimed at all forms of illegitimate authority ("No gods, no masters!"), is directed predominantly but nonexclusively against the state. The state is viewed as a higher, particularly powerful and vicious form of illegitimate authority.

From the perspective adopted here, it could be said that this theory is either very old or very recent.

Very old, to the extent that some aspects of anarchism can be discovered—with remarkable consistency—in authors, and in social and political movements, far removed from us in time and space. This pattern in fact leads some anarchists to hazard, somewhat daringly perhaps, that anarchism is a constant in human history precisely because it puts into play essential and fundamental facts of our "nature." Whatever the case, certain stateless societies described by contemporary anthropologists—the Essenes, Anabaptists and individuals as diverse as Lao Tse, Diogenes, Zeno, Spartacus, Étienne de La Boétie, Thomas Müntzer, François Rabelais, Gerrard Winstanley, Denis Diderot, and Jonathan Swift—are counted by anarchists as among their natural precursors. To limit myself to a single example, Diogenes, that cynic of Greek antiquity and proponent of fraternity and rationalism, was offered absolutely anything he could desire by the powerful Alexander the Great. He answered from his barrel, "Get out of my sunlight." This guy Diogenes seems quite like a distant ancestor of the anarchist.

However, anarchism is also a much more recent fact of history; an explicit and coherent formulation only arrived with the French Revolution. The very word "anarchism" only appeared for the first time in the writings of Pierre-Joseph Proudhon in the nineteenth century. Since then, many writers, traditions, and events have marked the history of anarchism. That is precisely the subject of this book.

The black flag (and, sometimes, a red and black flag) and Circle "A" are two universally recognized symbols of anarchism. However, their origins remain uncertain.

The black flag seems to have made one of its first appearances at the Paris Commune, with Louise Michel waving it at the head of a demonstration.

The symbol soon became identified with the anarchists: from the beginning of the 1880s, several anarchist organizations adopted it in the titles of their journals (*Black Flag*, 1881) or the names of their organizations (Black Flag International, 1882). It then became a regular feature of anarchist demonstrations and was present at all the landmarks of the movement: the black flag flew in Chicago after 1884; the Makhnovists fought under its banner in the Ukraine; and thousands of anarchists followed the black flag at Kropotkin's funeral on February 13, 1921, the date marking the end of anarchism in Soviet Russia.

It has been invested with diverse meanings. For some, it is a symbol of hunger, poverty, or the workers' revolt; for others, it symbolizes (dried) blood, shed by the "propaganda by the deed." The black flag could also have referred to pirates—rebels without a homeland whose flag was a declaration of their intent to fight enemies to the death.

Reviewing these diverse potential meanings, Howard Ehrlich perceives a symbol of negation—of the fury, outrage, beauty, and hope that anarchists are proud to bear, though they despair of it—against the day when this symbol is no longer useful. But we could also see it as the negation of the colors of all other flags.

The Circle "A"

Much newer to the history of anarchism, the Circle A was invented in Paris in 1964 . . . and then reinvented in Milan in 1966. This story is a bit complicated but typically anarchist, with neither centralized location nor individuals profiting from its invention, symbolically or financially.

The Circle A first appeared on the cover of the *Jeunes libertaires* (*Anarchist Youth*) newsletter in April 1964. The logo was proposed by the group of "Anarchist Youth (JL)" of Paris "for the entire anarchist movement." The group explains in the newsletter:

> Two main motivations have guided us: first, to facilitate and increase the efficiency of the concrete actions of applying graffiti and affixing posters; and next to provide the anarchist movement with a greater visual presence through a symbol shared by all expressions of anarchism in public demonstrations. Specifically, we needed to find a practical means of minimizing the time it takes to write by avoiding adding a long signature under our slogans, and, at the same time, to find a logo general enough that it can be adopted, used by all anarchists. The logo adopted seems to us to best meet these criteria. By constant association with the word anarchist, it will, through well-known mental association, come to spontaneously evoke the idea of anarchism in people's minds.

This capital "A" written inside a circle, designed by Tomás Ibañez and produced by René Darras, was used because it was easily produced and resembled the widely used peace sign of the Campaign for Nuclear Disarmament (CND). But this first proposal did not catch on, and the JL group disappeared or went into hibernation until May 1968.

Meanwhile, the Circle A was taken up again in 1966 by the *Gioventù libertaria de Milan,* who were in touch with the Anarchist Youth in Paris. It was thus in Milan that the sign first served as a signature for flyers and posters of anarchist youth before appearing throughout all of Italy and then the whole world. It did not reappear in France until the beginning of the 1970s, after which it spread rapidly.*

---

* Amadeo Bertolo and Marianne Enckell, "La véritable histoire du A cerclé (The True History of the Circle A)," *Bulletin du Centre international de recherches sur l'anarchisme* 58 (Mar.–Oct. 2002).

I. ROOTS

Some thinkers believe that anarchism is a permanent feature of human history, somehow written into human nature. Kropotkin, one of anarchism's most important thinkers, was of this opinion. In a famous introductory article on anarchism published in the Encyclopedia Britannica in 1910, he argued that a tension between a tendency toward anarchism and a tendency toward hierarchy runs throughout the course of human history.

Even if we accept this hypothesis of "eternal" anarchism, the appearance of a "historical" anarchism in the latter half of the nineteenth century would still need to be explained. How did it arise? What factors led to the numerous and varied forms anarchism assumed from that time? These questions are made less easy to answer by the fact that anarchism encompasses a rich and varied current of thought. Moreover, in retracing its history, we must cite the main social and political movements over the last two centuries, as well as most of the great currents of thought that shaped Europe—and then the rest of the world—during the same period.

Anarchism borrowed from many of these currents and most of these movements contributed to it. It is thus not surprising that a host of genealogies of anarchism are on offer. Before broaching the question of the sources of historical anarchism, let us recall its main trends. These are sometimes very far removed from each other and even, in certain cases or at least on certain levels, contradictory.

Since the nineteenth century, individualist anarchism and social anarchism have been easily distinguishable as two distinct trends. Individualist anarchism was first introduced and defended by Max Stirner. Outside the United States, where its offspring are many and diverse, individualist anarchism has not had the historical importance of social anarchism. To be fair, it has nevertheless contributed significantly to this archipelago of ideas that is anarchism.

Most anarchists fall under the umbrella of social anarchism, but distinctions must still be made among collectivists, federalists, communists, and syndicalists. These nuances arise over the means of attaining the ideal that is sought as well as the definition of the ideal itself. I will return to each of these subtleties at length.

The twentieth century witnessed a flowering of new ideas and directions in anarchism—all possible perspectives on the themes and nuances of thought and action. Let's review the main trends.

Leo Tolstoy introduced religious anarchism. At first glance, this is astonishing, because anarchism has generally been atheist, or at least agnostic; moreover, anarchism, and particularly Bakunin's anarchism, is one of the most radically anticlerical philosophies humanity has ever known.

Anarcho-pacifism was also inspired in part by Tolstoy. Magnificently defended by Ferdinand Domela Nieuwenhuis during the First World War, anarcho-pacifism has had several offshoots.

Anarcho-feminism, whose most notable proponent was Emma Goldman, assumed increasing importance throughout the twentieth century and is particularly influential in our era.

Anarcho-syndicalism was an important and fruitful movement. Ecological anarchism, of which Murray Bookchin is the best-known representative, is currently prominent. To Bookchin we also owe the recent school of libertarian municipalism.

To conclude this quick overview, there is currently a bitter dispute in North America between the various tendencies cited above and anarcho-capitalists, who identify with anarchism (falsely, according to the former) and particularly with individualist anarchism.

It is not surprising, then, that the sources of anarchism are as numerous and varied as the movement itself, and that many concurrent genealogies can be proposed.

Of the various readings of history, I will rely here on those of Henri Arvon and Noam Chomsky, which I find particularly illuminating.

Arvon presents the most widely accepted position. He situates anarchism in the fallout of the French Revolution—that is, in a mass revolutionary movement. It is an attractive perspective, because the entire history of anarchism has been punctuated with such movements, which in many respects have served both as engine and source of inspiration. However, the reference to the French Revolution reflects a certain state of civilization and formulation of social and political problems. Put simply, the argument is as follows: the French Revolution brought to fruition a movement of modernity whose roots dated back to the Renaissance (more or less) in the West and which sought to problematize the conditions of state legitimacy and, more generally, political power.

This movement, marked by various theories (social contract theory, natural law, divine right, etc.), was also crucially accompanied by the progressive empowerment and development of the individual. In sum, the contention here is that the French Revolution was able to expose, in an exemplary and emblematic way, the contradiction between the state—with its abstract celebration of liberty, equality, and fraternity—and society, which the state falsely claims to serve, and which is characterized by economic and other forms of inequality, including the servitude of some to others, and the struggle of each against all.

What does anarchism mean in this context? It is an antiauthoritarian and antistate reaction that suppresses the contradiction between state and society by radically denying one of those two terms: the state. Anarchism thus imagines a society without a state; a free union of free, equal, and fraternal beings. Born of an awareness of the contradiction between state and society that emerged during the French Revolution, anarchism is thus, in its negative dimension, the desire to abolish the state, and, in its positive dimension, the desire to construct a free, equal, and fraternal society.

This thesis is supported by the fact that demands for direct democracy, freedom, and real equality were in fact explicitly formulated during the French Revolution. A notable example of this is the Conspiracy of Equals faction, associated with Gracchus Babeuf (1760–1797): "Get rid of the revolting distinctions between rich and poor, the great and the lowly, the masters, the governors and the governed." Perhaps even more notable is the example of the *Enragé* (the Enraged), whom the French government of the time (the *Directoire*) rightly called "anarchists." Jacques Roux is their best-known figure: "The despotism of the Senate is just as terrible as the sceptre of kings. It enchains people without their knowledge; brutalizes them and subjugates them through laws that they are supposed to have conceived."

This historical reconstruction is convenient, but it seems to me to obscure an important part of what has given anarchism certain of its characteristics. We will turn to Noam Chomsky, who offers another genealogy of anarchism, to complement this account.

According to Chomsky, an essential aspect of the anarchist principle, and one of its most significant forms, can be found in Mikhail Bakunin. Specifically, Chomsky highlights Bakunin's praise of liberty as an essential condition for the opening and development of "human intelligence, dignity, and happiness."

Anarchism has developed a concept of freedom opposed to the freedom authorized and circumscribed by the state. A much broader and infinitely richer definition of freedom is proposed. Not confined to fixed limits, this freedom is not reduced to the exclusively negative liberty of not being impeded. On the contrary, it expands infinitely, as oppressive structures are discovered. Anarchism thus requires struggle against new limits on freedom, which are endlessly brought to light. Chomsky expresses this by introducing anarchism as "a tendency in the history of human thought and action which seeks to identify coercive, authoritarian, and hierarchic structures of all kinds and to challenge their legitimacy—and if they cannot justify their legitimacy, which is quite commonly the case, to work to undermine them and expand the scope of freedom."

Moreover, according to Chomsky, these ideas should also be linked to seventeenth century rationalism and particularly to René Descartes who, as we shall see, inspired Chomsky's reworking of linguistics.

Chomsky also argues very persuasively that these are Enlightenment ideas, notably expressed by Jean-Jacques Rousseau (1712–1778) in his *Discourse on the Origin of Inequality Among Men*, and Wilhelm von Humboldt (1767–1835) in *The Limits of State Action*. The concept of freedom that emerged in this era was articulated by Immanuel Kant (1724–1804), who said that liberty is "the precondition for the acquisition of the maturity necessary for the exercise of freedom and not a gift only received once this maturity has been acquired."

In an original and illuminating way, Chomsky finally ties anarchism to the ideas of eighteenth-century liberalism, "to the classical liberalism, which would be shattered by industrial capitalism and replaced by the ideological reconstruction of our times." In his view, anarchism came out of the liberals' opposition to state and church, which led progressively to the socialist ideal and then, becoming more radical, to the anarchist ideal: to libertarian socialism simultaneously advocating freedom and equality. We thus return to Bakunin: "Freedom without socialism leads to privileges and injustice; socialism without freedom leads to slavery and brutality."

However, there is a final source of anarchism, passed over by both accounts, which contributed not only to the appearance of these ideas but particularly to the form they assumed during the latter half of the nineteenth century.

This is the philosophy of Georg Wilhelm Friedrich Hegel (1770–1831). This German philosopher developed an ambitious (and, in my view, verbose and unnecessarily obscure) system leading to a synthesis, called philosophical idealism, strongly marked by Christianity, monarchy, and bourgeois culture. After Hegel died, some of his dissident followers, known as "leftist" Hegelians, began to dismantle this synthesis, attacking each aspect. Where Hegel describes the progressive discovery of the transcendence of the Spirit, his young disciples posit the immanence of the human mind, progressively gaining self-consciousness. For Ludwig Feuerbach (1804–1872), religion was no more than "the relation of man to himself" and theology supplanted by anthropology. Stirner's individualist anarchism was a radicalization of this perspective, accepting no horizon but the "I," the "Unique One." Moreover, as we shall see, Bakunin, and from that point onward a significant part of social anarchism, was also influenced by Hegelianism.

We can conclude with the idea of the dialectic. Hegel defines it as follows in his *Logic*: "To study things in their own being and movement and thus to demonstrate the finitude of the partial categories of understanding." The dialectic is simultaneously the movement of the real and of the thought grasping it, there being an identity between the two in Hegel's idealist system. The dialectic is often simply presented as a triad whose three points are: assertion—negation—negation of the negation (or new assertion), which will in its turn be negated and so on.

To conclude this foray into the subject, I'll relate a famous anecdote. In November 1889, in Barcelona, there was a fiery debate between communist anarchists and collectivist anarchists on the relative merits of their positions. Fernando Tarrida del Mármol, a Cuban exile, brought it to an end by calling for tolerance. Once it is understood that the primary goal of all anarchists is to abolish capitalism and the state and to experiment freely in order to establish a free society, he said, one should practice what can be called a theoretical tolerance toward secondary differences of perspective. Marmol concluded with the now-famous expression, "Anarchism without adjectives."

Put simply, anarchism is not a patented idea, and thankfully so; there are no property rights over the concept. It remains an open theory, destined for further transformations. I would contend that anarchism is only alive and worthy of interest to the extent that it remains open to change.

2. ANARCHISTS AND ANARCHISM

William Godwin and Rationalism

We have presented numerous forerunners of anarchism. In addition to those already cited, a special place should be reserved for Gerrard Winstanley, who, in *The Law of Freedom* (1652), developed ideas akin to those later advanced by anarchists. It is generally accepted, however, that anarchism was first formulated by William Godwin (1756–1836) in *An Enquiry Concerning Political Justice*, published in 1793. Godwin and early feminist activist Mary Wollstonecraft had a daughter, also named Mary, who is best known as the author of the novel *Frankenstein*. The younger Mary married the poet Percy Bysshe Shelley, who greatly contributed to the spread of anarchist ideas. Godwin, believing in both absolute determinism and human perfectibility, was a rationalist: believing that "Man is a rational being," he wrote: "Reason is the only legislator, and her decrees are irrevocable and uniform."

Because Godwin believed that people are shaped by their environment, his writings are greatly concerned with education and, more generally, with all forces of rational persuasion. Godwin thought these could bring about a just society by transforming the environment (type of government and education; social and religious prejudices) to eliminate elements impeding the full exercise of reason. For at least three reasons, Godwin fully deserves the place he holds in the history of anarchism. First of all, a consistent antiauthoritarianism runs throughout his work; this is apparent in his refusal to accept the dictates of tradition, sensation, sentiment, and habit without first subjecting them to the test of reason. His defense of rationalism is also a major characteristic of anarchism. Finally, Godwin concludes with an antistate position, formulating the contradiction between state and society as follows: "Society is produced by our wants, and government by our wickedness. Society is in every state a blessing; government in its best state but a necessary evil." Godwin's anarchism thus paved the way for social anarchism, which Bakunin and Kropotkin in particular would develop. However, before reaching that point, the anarchist position was profoundly influenced by a German philosopher.

Max Stirner's Egoism and Associationism

Max Stirner (1806–1856) is the pseudonym of Johann Kaspar Schmidt. Born in 1806 in Bayreuth, Bavaria, he studied philosophy at the University of Berlin from 1826 to 1828, where he was decisively influenced by Hegel. In 1832, he began working toward a teaching degree and, after several difficult years, obtained a teaching position at a boarding school for young girls in Berlin.

This "respectable" position explains why Professor Schmidt

soon adopted the pseudonym Max Stirner to sign his writings. Stirner wrote very little. Apart from a few articles published in the *Rheinische Zeitung* (*The Rhenish Gazette*), edited at the time by Karl Marx, and a few other minor works, Stirner produced just one book, *Der Einzige und sein Eigentum* (*The Ego and Its Own*). Published in 1845, it was a powerful, radical, and profoundly original work. Stirner wrote it when he was a member of *Die Freien* (the Free), a group of leftist Hegelians that included Marx and Friedrich Engels. (Marx and Engels devoted lengthy passages of *The German Ideology* to a critique of *The Ego*, which they saw as the idealism of a petit bourgeois who refused to move beyond barren speculation and the purely theoretical into practice.)

Stirner died, a complete unknown, in 1856. The Scottish-born German poet and novelist John Henry Mackay rescued him from obscurity with his 1898 work *Max Stirner, sein Leben und sein Werk* (*Max Stirner: His Life and His Work*), the first exhaustive study of the philosopher. *The Ego* became the bible of individualist anarchists and has enjoyed a constant readership—not large, but always enthusiastic.

Stirner argues that the "I" is unique and irreducible to the realities and categories in which we attempt to imprison it. The 'I' can consider everything else as its own. "God and humanity based their cases on themselves alone. Therefore, I will base my case on myself: just as much as God, I am the negation of everything else; for myself, I am all in all; I am the Unique One."

The I is considered indefinable—any definition would categorize it, which cannot be done without mutilating it.

This perspective stems from a radical critique of leftist Hegelian positions; especially of Feuerbach, whose critique of religion led to the "anthropologization" of theology, God, and religion. Stirner rebels: this is to create a new idol, humanity, to which the I must still subject itself.

Stirner's critique extends to revolutionary positions that would subject the Ego to the dictatorship of abstract categories: deified society, to which we owe submission and obedience; the state, which, according to Stirner, "has only one aim: to restrict, dominate, master the individual and subordinate him to the general"; or revolution, that last incarnation of deified society, of the general, of the collective—and a new pretext to oppress the I. "When a communist salutes you as man and brother, he is speaking from his Sunday profession of faith. On regular days, he doesn't see you simply as a man, but as a human worker or a working man. The first is inspired by liberal principles; in the second is concealed its anti-liberal nature. If you were an idler, he certainly wouldn't fail to recognize the man in you, but he would strive to purify it, as the slothful man. He would attempt to convert you to the belief that work is the destiny and vocation of man."

The I, therefore, must undertake the long labor of reappropriation of the self and discovery of its own uniqueness. It must extricate itself from the dross of general and abstract ideas in which all conspire to imprison it.

Nothing escapes from this virulent critique: "Religion, morality, God, conscience, Party, duties and all those stupidities with which brain and heart are stuffed." It is notable that Stirner's analysis of education remains as powerful as ever and his ideals are still stimulating: "Youth are herded into schools and once they have memorized the verbiage of the old, they are declared to be of age. . . . All education must become personal—it is not about inculcating knowledge, but achieving the full blossoming of the personality. . . . The starting point of pedagogy should not be to civilize but to train free personalities, independent characters."

Taking the critique to its conclusion, Stirner suggests refounding social life on the basis of associationism, conceived of a meeting of freely and voluntarily associated egoists. Such relations, which can be broken off at any time, allow the I to maintain its independence and uniqueness. For Stirner, they are the only natural and acceptable ones.

Individualists, Stirner's followers, have always marked the history of anarchism. At the turn of the century, during the so-called Belle Époque, they were numerous and made themselves highly visible, notably by advocating sexual liberation and practicing "individual reappropriation," which society called "theft."

They seemed to have taken Proudhon's slogan literally: "Property is theft." In practice, however, reappropriation of what the rich have confiscated raises certain questions. Errico Malatesta responded as follows in *Umanità Nova* on July 11, 1922:

> Do anarchists recognize theft? Two things must be distinguished. If a man wants to work and can't find work, and thus would be reduced to dying from hunger amidst wealth, it is indisputably his right to take what he needs from those who have more than enough. And if other people's lives depend on this man—children, the sick, defenseless old people—it can even become a duty. But if it is a case of theft to avoid the necessity of working, with the

aim of creating capital and living off it, it is clear that anarchists do not accept ownership, which is successful theft, consolidated, legalized, used as a means of exploiting the labor of others. They therefore can't commit theft, which is embryonic ownership. He who does not work lives by exploiting the labor of others, whether directly as an industrialist or indirectly as a thief . . . or rentier.

We don't condemn the individual, not even thieves and not even capitalists. We understand the inevitability of current social conditions, of social position, of education; and that's why we want to destroy the system that enables theft and capitalism, which are, in the end, one and the same thing.

This conclusion is echoed by Georges Brassens (1921–1981)—better known for his songs than his anarchist convictions—who wrote under the name "Pépin le Bref" in the anarchist press. The "Postscript" in his *Stances à un cambrioleur* (*Stanzas for a Burglar*) read, "If theft is your preferred art, your sole vocation, your one talent, establish yourself, take up business, and you will have even cops among your frequent customers."

However, if we agree with Murray Bookchin that anarchism largely developed by working this tension between Stirner's personal development and the tendency that strives, on the contrary, to promote social freedom, its bases and collective conditions, it must be admitted that Stirner's egoism and associationism have played a significant role in the development of anarchist thought.

A flamboyant figure of the anarchist world, Albert Libertad (1875–1908) had two disabled legs and made good use of his crutches in brawls—in which he participated relatively often. An excellent journalist, he wrote for the Parisian anarchist press, particularly *Le Libertaire* (*The Libertarian*) and Sébastien Faure's daily *Le Journal du peuple* (*People's Daily*). In 1902, he initiated a *Causeries populaires* (popular discussion) group to popularize his ideas and also helped found an antimilitarist league. On April 13, 1905, the first issue of his own weekly, *L'Anarchie* (*Anarchy*), was published. To the youthful Victor Kibalchich (also known as Victor Serge, and at the time writing under the name "Le Rétif" [the Rebel]), Libertad was "the soul of an extraordinarily dynamic movement." He summed up its doctrine as, "Don't wait for the revolution. Those who promote the revolution are jokers just like the rest. Make your own revolution."

After his death, the movement Libertad had founded faltered amid many sterile attempts, due to being, as le Rétif wrote, "both individualist (push yourself to be a new man) and revolutionary (duty and necessity of participating in the class struggle)." Not until the 1960s did some of the themes tried out and popularized by Libertad's friends resurface, such as free love, communes, and the will to live another life immediately, here and now.

Let's conclude with Émile Armand, undoubtedly the most famous of the individualist anarchists. Until his death in 1962, Armand spread his ideas through journals (especially *L'en-dehors* [*Outside*]) and books that provoked scandals, especially over their advocacy of sexual freedom. It was Armand who penned the famous line, "Marriage is long-term prostitution; prostitution short-term marriage."

Pierre-Joseph Proudhon and Mutualism

Pierre-Joseph Proudhon (1809–1865) was born of humble origins in Besançon, in the region of Franche-Comté, France, in 1809. He was forced early on, for lack of money, to interrupt his studies and become a printer. "I know what poverty is," he later wrote. "I lived it. Everything I know, I owe to despair."

In 1838, he received a grant from the Academy of Besançon, which allowed him to go to Paris to work on a book. Published in 1840, *Qu'est-ce que la propriété?* (*What is Property?*) created a scandal. His grant was withdrawn, but he won the admiration and esteem of the young Marx. The book included the famous phrase, "Property is theft," and for the first time used the term "anarchism" to describe the political position since known by that name. The following passages are very famous and deserve to be quoted at length:

> If I had to answer the question, "What is slavery?" in a single word, I'd say: it's murder. My thinking would be understood immediately. I wouldn't need to make a long speech to explain that the power to seize a person's thought, will, personality is a power of life and death, and to enslave a man is to assassinate him. So in response to this other question, "What is property?," why is it not possible to respond likewise, "It's theft," without feeling certain of not being understood, even though the second claim is only a transformation of the first?

Further:

You are a republican.

—Republican, yes, but the word says nothing. *Res publica* means the public thing. Anyone who wants the public thing, under any form of government at all, can call themselves republican. Kings are also republicans.

—Okay then! You are a democrat?

—No.

—What! You are a monarchist?

—No.

—Constitutional?

—God forbid.

—So an aristocrat?

—Not in the least.

—You want a mixed government?

—Even less so.

—So what are you?

—I am an anarchist.

—I get it: you are being satirical, this is directed at the government.

—Certainly not: you just heard my serious and long reflected profession of faith; while a great friend of order, I am, in the full meaning of the term, anarchist.

Once again without means, Proudhon left to work in Lyons in 1840. He continued to publish texts, which assured his ever-increasing popularity—but also trouble with the law. During this period he conceived of mutual credit institutions, workers' cooperatives, and the whole associative movement to which his name remains attached.

Proudhon supported the revolution in February 1848, though with some reservations and nuances. That same year, he launched the first anarchist newspaper, *Le Représentant du peuple* (*The People's Representative*), and he was elected to the National Assembly. In January 1849, he created the People's Bank, which the authorities soon closed. Proudhon was exiled. After he returned to France, he was sentenced to prison, where he remained for three years.

In 1851, he published *The General Idea of the Revolution in the Nineteenth Century*, which advocated an ideal anarchist society based on contracts freely consented to and the idea of freely federated communes. He then called himself a federalist.

In 1858, Proudhon was again condemned to prison and fled to Belgium. He returned to France in 1862. From then on, the mutualism and federalism he advocated became forces to be reckoned with. Proudhon died in 1865, but not before he became aware of the important role his ideas played in the newly formed International.

Some have written that Proudhon's work is a kind of pot-luck: people only find what they have brought to it in the first place. This is an exaggeration, just like the view that Proudhon's work is completely contradictory. However, his thought is sometimes complex and subtle. This is particularly true around the question of property. Proudhon condemned property while defending a precise form of it: possession. It must be admitted that on some issues his perspectives are very surprising, even inconsistent in certain respects. "God is evil," wrote the ferociously "anti-theist" Proudhon, who created the word to describe his position. Nevertheless, he raised his daughters as Christians.

The deplorable and inexcusable sexism of this advocate of freedom and equality has also rightly been pointed out.

Proudhon was in fact a nonsystematic thinker who distrusted absolutes and definitive answers. His thought is rooted in an antiauthoritarianism that revolts against government, power, state, laws, and suffrage (even universal) as so many means of "oppressing and exploiting others." But Proudhon's central issue, the key to all the rest, is economic. For Proudhon, the conditions for an anarchist society should be sought in the first place through economic transformation. Summing up this project, he wrote that he aimed to "melt, submerge, and make the political or governmental system disappear in the economic system; by reducing, simplifying, decentralizing, and destroying, one by one, each cog of that great machine called government."

He holds the capitalist economy and—before Marx—its exploitive nature primarily responsible:

> Capitalism pays for workers' days. To be exact, the capitalist pays as many times over for one day that it employs workers each day—which is not at all the same thing. The capitalist has not paid for the immense power resulting from the action and harmony of the workers; the convergence and simultaneity of their efforts. Two hundred soldiers installed the Luxor Obelisk on its pedestal. Could a single man have done this in two hundred days? However, according to the capitalist's reckoning, the total salaries are the same.

Proudhon's rejection of property is a refusal to acknowledge the authority of an unjust mode of appropriation, made possible by a specific model of economic organization. He does not reject the idea of possession, understood as the free disposal of the legitimate returns on one's labor, paid in the form of labor bonds. "All human labor necessarily resulting from collective effort, all property becomes, by the same token, collective and indivisible. More precisely, labor destroys property." Proudhon wavered on the exact calculation of these returns, but remained constant on the principle of a distinction between property and possession: "Individual possession is the condition of social life; five thousand years of property show that it is suicidal for society. Possession is lawful; property unlawful."

It has been noted many times that Proudhon's economic doctrine is tightly linked to the practices of peasants, small craftspeople, and independent shopkeepers. This is largely true, and Proudhon does not conceal it. "The constitutive unit of society is the workshop," he writes, adding that in the anarchist commune, "the workshop will replace government."

But his most significant contributions to economics, those which have had the greatest historical impact, do not lie with his undoubtedly nostalgic attachment to the workshop. Rather, his originality and lasting interest is found in his writings on mutualism, which prefigure the cooperative movement, and the idea of self-organization, which he was the first to propose with such force and conviction. Proudhon imagined people's banks, dispensing interest-free loans and accepting labor bonds as payment. Moreover, workers would be associated in production units they possessed and managed themselves, as equals. While mutualism and self-organization allow economic emancipation and well-being, federalism ensures political emancipation. "Free association, freedom, which is bound to maintain equality in the means of production and equivalence in exchanges, is the only possible, just, real form of society. The political is the science of freedom: government of man by man, however it masks itself, is oppression; the highest perfection of society lies in the union of order and anarchy."

Like freely undertaken contracts between producers, the political contract binds the contractors—commune, canton, province—by guaranteeing them greater rights and freedoms than they yield. According to Proudhon, in such a society—and only in such a society—each person becomes "his own autocrat." At that point, "powerful and weak no longer exist; there are only workers, whose aptitudes and means will continue to move towards equalization, through individual solidarity and the guarantee of mobility."

Antiauthoritarianism, antistatism, egalitarianism, mutualism, federalism, self-organization: anarchism would later distinguish among these positions. However, for having articulated these various positions within a fundamentally coherent whole, Proudhon undoubtedly deserves the title generally attributed to him of being the founder of anarchism. Bakunin, despite unquestionably moving away from Proudhon's positions, still rightly called him "the master of us all."

Mikhail Bakunin and Federalism
Mikhail Bakunin (1814–1876) was born into the nobility in Russia. His father, a disciple of Jean-Jacques Rousseau and his pedagogical ideas, took charge of his son's primary edu-

cation. Bakunin later attended the Mikhailovskaya Artillery Military School in Saint Petersburg, embarking on a military career until his love of literature led him in a different direction in 1835.

He then became absorbed in German philosophy; first Johann Gottlieb Fichte, then Hegel. In 1840, he moved to Berlin to study philosophy and in 1842 began to frequent the leftist Young Hegelians. Under the influence of one of them, Arnold Ruge, he believed that the Hegelian dialectic could and should be put to the service of the revolution and not reaction, following Hegel's example. Bakunin celebrated the negative point of the Hegelian triad, the moment of revolt and destruction, "the joy of destruction is at the same time a creative joy." The radical positions that he was then taking in Europe in support of the Slavs and Poles earned him, *in absentia*, a sentence of exile by Russia. Bakunin thereafter lived in Belgium, but went to France in 1848 to support the revolution.

He joined in all struggles—and not just in writing. He was on the barricades and fomented plots and conspiracies. Described as a giant of limitless energy, he threw himself into the revolution without reserve. Condemned to death in Saxony and Austria, he was finally handed over to the Russian authorities in 1849. In 1857, he was sent to Siberia. He escaped in 1861 and undertook a long and perilous journey that took him from Japan to the United States and back to Europe.

By this time, Bakunin's thought was undeniably and completely anarchist; but he never ceased, even as he developed his ideas, to feed his insatiable appetite for action. In 1863, he participated with the Poles in an unsuccessful invasion of Lithuania, finally fleeing to Italy; in Naples in 1865, he organized an International Fraternity and then a League of Peace and Freedom; in 1868, he founded the International Alliance of Socialist Democracy, which he dissolved the same year in order to join Marx and the First International. The conflicts that later pitted him against Marx— along with delegates from southern Europe (the Italian, Spanish, and Jurassian federations, the French federation having been barred after the 1871 Commune)—were epic. They were about the essence, meaning, and means of revolutionary action and theory.

In 1872, the Hague Congress expelled Bakunin from the International. Two years earlier, he had taken part in the Lyons Commune; in 1874, he participated in the Bologna rebellion. But his health was failing, and in 1876, he died in Bern.

Bakunin's anarchism is based on the idea of a progressive humanization of the species through the exercise of reason. Reason discovers, little by little, the laws of nature, and by this means establishes and makes possible an ever-expanding freedom in proportion to the degree to which humanization is attained. It has often been pointed out that these ideas owe a great deal to Hegel, Auguste Comte, Marx, and Proudhon. Bakunin's originality, however, lies elsewhere, chiefly in three aspects: his adamant atheism and anticlericalism; his remarkably accurate critique of what he called authoritarian socialism; and the definition of federalism as the architecture of an anarchist society and world.

Bakunin saw the developments of religion as one of the great stages in of the humanization of the species. Nonetheless, he also believed that it was time to end what he called "divine slavery," now become an obstacle to human-ization, the ultimate source of all authority and the basis of all other forms of slavery.

"All temporal and human authority derives from spiritual or divine authority," he wrote. "But authority is the negation of freedom. God, or rather the fiction of God, is thus the con-secration and the moral and intellectual cause of all slavery on earth, and man's freedom will never be complete until it has completely annihilated the fiction of a heavenly master." The scandalous syllogism summarizing this perspective is well known. "If there is a God, man is a slave; however, man can and must be free, thus God does not exist."

His revolt next turned against the state, the "little brother of the church" and another "historically necessary evil," also destined to disappear. Ferociously antiauthoritarian, Bakunin delivered a fierce attack on all states, including those claiming to exercise power in the interests of the oppressed majority: "We renounce all law, all authority, all privileged, patented, official, and legal influence, even the outcome of universal suffrage, convinced that it can never lead to anything but the benefit of a dominant and exploit-ative minority over the interests of the vast subjugated majority. This is what makes us anarchists."

This was in fact the central point in the bitter confron-tation that pitted anarchists against Marxists and com-munists—"authoritarian socialists"—in the First Interna-tional.

Bakunin predicted that the dictatorship of the proletariat, so dear to the communists, would not lead to the withering of the state (a claim he viewed as the "most vile and dan-gerous lie our century has given rise to"), but could only engender a new and frightening tyranny, a "red bureau-cracy," which he saw as inevitable. History has amply confirmed his prediction. "Take the most radical revolu-tionary," Bakunin elaborated, "and place him on the throne of all the Russias or grant him dictatorial power . . . within a year, he will have become worse than the Tsar."

The federalism he espouses engages ideas that merit attention. Clearly influenced by the romanticism of his era, Bakunin believed that this mode of non-state social organi-zation would be achieved through a sudden, spontaneous revolt. While recognizing the importance of collective labor action—his thinking partly prefigures anarcho-syndi-calism, as we will see below—and advocating affinity-group action against the status quo, Bakunin put his money on the spontaneity of the masses.

This destructive phase would sweep away the old institu-tions—church, state, judicial apparatus, banks, army, etc. (including inheritance, especially of land)—and establish a free and egalitarian society. This would ensure that all members of society, now educated and freed from eco-nomic constraints, could participate in common affairs: "All individuals, men and women, enter life with more or less equal means to develop their different faculties and to put them to use through their labor." He further writes that it is a matter of "organizing a society which, making it impossible for any individual, whoever it be, to exploit the labor of others, allows each person to participate in the enjoyment of social riches that he contributes to produce through his own labor."

Inverting the dominant model of representative democ-racy, political organization takes place from the bottom up, through direct democracy, with freely federating individuals. The federative principle progressively links "the free federation of individuals in communes, communes in provinces, provinces in nations, these into the United States of Europe and then the entire world." Bakunin devoted lengthy passages to the functioning of these federated entities. Beyond these descriptions and their share of utopia, the spirit infusing these pages is remarkable.

Bakunin developed a very rich concept of liberty, linked to solidarity: the liberty of each person is not limited by the liberty of others, but finds in the liberty of others the possibility of infinite expansion. "The law of social solidarity is the first human law; liberty is the second. These two laws are intertwined and, being inseparable, they constitute the essence of humanity. Liberty is not the essence of solidarity, but its development and, so to speak, humanization."

While Bakunin was not as powerful or original a thinker as Marx, Proudhon, or Kropotkin, his conception of liberty and solidarity still deserves our full attention: "I am not fully free until all other people around me, men and women, are also free; the more numerous are the free individuals surrounding me, the deeper and wider their freedom, the more extensive, deeper, and wider mine becomes."

Peter Kropotkin and Anarcho-Communism

Peter Kropotkin (1842–1921) is one of the most attractive figures of the anarchist movement. Countless people who knew him praised his great humanity. The last great voice of classical anarchism, Kropotkin was a scholar admired by his peers. He was a geographer who made significant academic contributions to his discipline as well as to anthropology, history, biology, and sociology. Above all, he was the most ardent promoter of anarcho-communism and the most profound anarchist thinker, attempting to give anarchism a scientific basis.

Born into Russian high nobility (a prince at birth), Kropotkin was a page in the Tsar's court and began a military career, as he recounts in *Memoirs of a Revolutionist.* However, he soon came under the strong influence of liberal writing, which was then proliferating in Russia. This led him to seek a transfer to Siberia at the beginning of the 1860s. There he hoped to have a greater chance to "serve humanity."

Kropotkin used his stay to gather scientific data, which he relied on to make some of his most notable contributions to physical geography. At the same time, he studied the Russian penitentiary system, which disgusted him. Later he spent many years in prison himself and wrote several texts on the terrible consequences of the prison system and the need for reform. In 1865, however, he was still free in Siberia, reading Proudhon and becoming acquainted with anarchist ideas.

The following year, he left the army in protest over the execution of Polish fugitives. Over the next years, in Russia and in Europe, Kropotkin devoted himself primarily to geography, a field in which he became a leading figure. In 1870, he turned to action and political theory. He communicated with representatives of various socialist ideologies, studying each. A visit to the anarchist watchmakers of Jura—the Jura Federation section of the First International, whose members were mostly watchmakers in Jura Mountains, Switzerland—convinced him; at that point, he became decisively anarchist.

Kropotkin then returned to Russia, where he engaged in revolutionary activities. He was arrested in 1874, escaping in 1876 in a spectacular and extravagant episode. He then returned to Europe and entered an intense, ten-year period of propaganda and activism. Expelled from Switzerland at the request of the Russian government in September 1881, Kropotkin took refuge first in Thonon-les-Bains (Haute-Savoie), and then in England. Returning to Thonon in October 1882, he was arrested with sixty other anarchists on December 20, even though he was an outsider to the events that were then unfolding. It was a climate of social crisis—a miners' strike in Montceau-les-Mines and a crisis in the silk industry in Lyons—in which the class struggle was becoming increasingly violent. Power, as it is wont to do, sought scapegoats—in this case, among the anarchist activists.

The trial began on January 8, 1883, at a criminal court in Lyons. Kropotkin was sentenced to five years in prison, provoking strong international protest. He spent his time giving courses to his fellow detainees and writing a large number of academic articles, some of which were published in the *Encyclopedia Britannica*. Freed in 1886 under pressure by international public opinion, Kroptkin left for England. He remained there until 1917, when he returned to Russia to support the revolution.

These years witnessed his most significant theoretical contributions to anarchism. Prior to this, his writing had been circumstantial, tied to immediate action and specific events. In England, he systematized his views and, with new strength and rigor, developed the principles of anarcho-communism, which he advocated. He also tried to relate anarchist theory to the science of his times, aiming to provide it with a scientific grounding. This took him into sociology, economics, history, philosophy, and biology. His most remarkable work from this period was *Mutual Aid: A Factor of Evolution*. I will come back to this at length when I explore the moral positions of anarchists.

In 1916, Kropotkin drafted and signed the Manifesto of the Sixteen, which supported the Allies, and war. A major schism developed within the anarchist movement between the signatories of this text and anarchists who remained pacifist and internationalist. The Russian was denounced as a "government anarchist."

Kropotkin returned to Russia in 1917 as a famous scholar and an internationally respected intellectual. He hoped, briefly, that the nascent Russian Revolution would turn towards anarchism, carried along by the Soviets, the councils. He was very quickly disenchanted wrote in his April 1919 Letter to the Workers of Western Europe: "This state of war has been the pretext for strengthening dicta-torial methods which centralize the control of every detail of life in the hands of the government, with the effect of stopping an immense part of the ordinary activities of the country. . . . As long as the country is governed by a party dictatorship, the workers' and peasants' councils evidently lose their entire significance. . . . A coucil of workers ceases to be free and of any use when liberty of the press no longer exists, and we have been in that condition for two years . . ."

Kropotkin died on February 8, 1921, in the village of Dmitrov near Moscow. An impressive funeral was held the following Sunday. The authorities wanted to hold a national ceremony, but his loved ones refused. They demanded the liberation of some of the many anarchists imprisoned by the Bolsheviks, if only for the day. Kropotkin's funeral turned into a parade of thousands waving red or black flags. It was the last public anarchist demonstration in the USSR.

A monumental, unfinished work, *Ethics*, was published the following year.

After Stirner's associationism, Proudhon's mutualism, and Bakunin's federalism, Kropotkin's anarcho-communism is the last of the great models put forward by classical anarchism.

Most anarchists, while glad to depict the main contours of an anarchist society, were able to escape the accusations of utopianism leveled at them at any opportunity. However, most of them also refused to engage in what they considered to be the authoritarian, potentially counterproductive, and dangerous exercise of laying out precise and definite plans for this nonauthoritarian and non-statist society. As Kropotkin wrote, harmony in such a society would be achieved "by an incessant movement of adjustment and readjustment among a multitude of forces and influences." How it would work in detail could only be discovered through experimentation.

Kropotkin did not argue otherwise. However, his work shows a clear concern with establishing the viability of social organization freed from the constraints of illegitimate authority, as well as a sense of practical reality. This leads him to take a pragmatic approach to the various objections raised in response to anarchist solutions. In the field of economics, for example, Kropotkin elaborates the possible organization of an anarcho-communist society in great detail.

Kropotkin's historical research led him to argue that the

experiences of the French Revolution and the Commune showed that the illusion that representative government is necessary must be abandoned. The key to revolution henceforth became for him, as for the European anarchists, expropriation.

How is the economy to be conceived and organized after the big day when this is realized?

In *The Conquest of Bread* and *Fields, Factories and Workshops*, Kropotkin makes a convincing argument for the viability and efficacy of an economy conceptualized from the point of view of the consumers and of human need. There is obviously no place in such an economy for salary, even in the diluted form of "bonds"' that Proudhon retained. Instead, it works on the principle of "to each according to his or her needs," practicing *prise au tas* (literally, taken from the pile), with warehouses designated for the purpose. Reading these works is an unusual experience, because Kropotkin seems to have envisaged and responded in advance to many of the objections that one would be tempted to raise. Beyond the arguments, however, the reader is most struck by the high moral content of the thought and its sense of justice. "Everything is everyone's," wrote Kropotkin. "Because everyone has need, because everyone works according to their strength, and because it is materially impossible to determine how much belongs to each person in the current production of wealth." These remarkable books conclude: "Imagine a society of several million people, engaged in agriculture and a wide variety of industries. . . . Say . . . that every adult . . . commits to working five hours per day from the age of 20 or 22 until 45 or 50, in the occupation of their choice, in whatever area of human labor considered necessary. Such a society could guarantee in return the well-being of all its members, an affluence just as real as that enjoyed by today's bourgeoisie." Finally, and perhaps above all, Kropotkin holds that such a society would serve to satisfy not only the physical but also the artistic, intellectual, and moral needs of its members: "There are as many desires as there are individuals; the more civilized a society, the more individuality is developed and desires vary."

Kropotkin's spirit and values still inspire some contemporary anarchist studies and ideas in the field of economics. In particular, they are reflected in "participatory economics," which I examine below.

Some Successors

From Kropotkin, up through the time of Noam Chomsky, the anarchist movement produced a considerable number of thinkers and philosophers. However, none of these offered particularly notable innovations on the range of anarchist positions already available. Strong and attractive personalities nevertheless continued to emerge. I will note a few here, leaving aside for the moment the writers and activists whose contributions will be examined below.

RUSSIA

Emma Goldman (1869–1940), a prolific writer born in Russia who emigrated in 1885 to the United States, was a tireless advocate of anarchist ideas through her books, talks, and journal, *Mother Earth*. Along with others like Voltairine de Cleyre (1866–1912), she firmly integrated a feminist analysis, which soon took on increasing importance. Part of Goldman's work in this area consisted of advocating the use of contraception. She and her companion, Alexander Berkman, opposed the First World War. This landed them in prison in 1917 and led to their exile two years later. Leaving to discover the Russian Revolution, they were horrified by the police state established by Vladimir Lenin. Goldman immediately denounced the totalitarian bent of the Soviet regime in her remarkable *My Disillusionment in Russia* (1923). Berkman's *The ABC of Anarchism* (1929) remains one of the best introductions to anarchist ideas.

UNITED STATES

This era witnessed the development of a strong individualist current of anarchism in the United States, inspired by Stirner. Benjamin Tucker (1854–1939) and Lysander Spooner (1808–1887) are the best-known figures. This movement notably spawned a line of argument firmly opposed to taxation. Contemporary anarcho-capitalists try to link their position to the ideas of these writers, which are still bitterly controversial today. Henry David Thoreau (1817–1862), the pacifist who theorized civil disobedience, is also of note.

Anarchism took center stage in the United States twice during this period. The first time was in 1886, with the Haymarket affair [see page 66]. The second, starting in 1920, was related to the case of Sacco and Vanzetti, two anarchist workers from Italy who were arrested, detained for years, and then executed on August 23, 1927. Charged with stealing pay from the company they worked for, they never ceased to insist on their innocence. These two events sparked significant protest movements across the world.

Paul Goodman, a strong personality, wrote stimulating

reflections on education (*Compulsory Mis-education*, 1962; *The Community of Scholars*, 1964), which prefigured the tenets of the "deschooling" movement [see page 111].

ITALY

In Italy, Errico Malatesta (1853–1932) was only fourteen when he was arrested for the first time. He was accused of insulting the king in a letter he wrote to denounce an injustice. First a follower of Bakunin, he became closer to Kropotkin and advocated direct action and "propaganda of the deed." "Anarchism is born of a moral revolt against social injustice," he wrote. Its success is achieved "through the awakening consciousness of those habituated to obedience and passivity, to their real power and possibility." Malatesta moved into action in Bénévent in 1877, where he and his comrades distributed weapons to residents and burned the administrative archives. Maletesta was exiled and his life became one of travel, activism, launching magazines, and publishing manifestos, articles, and books. He put strong emphasis on the necessity of organizing anarchist groups. In 1907, the International Anarchist Congress was held in Amsterdam. He opposed Pierre Monatte (1881–1960) in a famous debate. The latter urged anarchists to join unions, an idea Malatesta strongly opposed: "We want an anarchist revolution that transcends the interests of a single class: it anticipates the liberation of all humanity, currently in economic, political, and moral slavery."

Malatesta returned to Italy for the first time in 1913. As protests in Ancona led to a general strike throughout the country, he organized the famous Red Week in 1914. Exiled again, he vigorously opposed what he considered the unspeakable treason of Kropotkin and the other signatories of the pro-war Manifesto of the Sixteen, which took up the cause of one imperialism against another. Malatesta argued that the internationalism of anarchists prohibited such a compromise.

He returned to Italy for the last time in 1919, where he took part in the factory occupation movement in 1920. Placed under house arrest by the Fascists in 1926, he was silenced and died six years later.

FRANCE

In France, Jean Grave (1854–1939), a self-educated cobbler, was centrally involved in *Le Révolté* (*Rebel*), *La Révolte* (*Revolt*), and then *Les Temps Nouveaux* (*The New Times*). The latter was published until 1914 and became a central forum for exchange among anarchist artists, writers, and activists.

Sébastien Faure (1858–1942) is one of the leading figures of French anarchism and pacifism. Opposed to anarcho-syndicalism, he believed in education as the means of promoting anarchism. He established a school, La Ruche, which was open for ten years, until 1914. A public speaker and the founder of periodicals and the newspaper *Le Libertaire* (*The Libertarian*), Faure was also the editor of the monumental *L'Encyclopédie anarchiste* (*The Anarchist Encyclopedia*) (1934).

Paul Robin (1837–1912) was also an educator: the founder and head of another renowned anarchist pedagogical experiment, Cempuis. Robin was also a strong advocate of birth control and neo-Malthusianism, a doctrine that attracted some anarchists for a time.

Élisée Reclus (1830–1905) directed *Le Révolté* (*Rebel*), the newspaper he founded with Kropotkin and Jean Grave. He is best remembered for his impressive *Géographie universelle* (*The Universal Geography*), which established his renown in that discipline, and for *La Nouvelle géographie universelle, la terre et les homes* (*The Earth and Its Inhabitants*).

Born in Aveyron, Émile Pouget (1860–1931) made a major contribution to the libertarian tone that influenced French syndicalism during the "heroic era." Close to Parisian anarchist groups from 1875 on, he was arrested in 1883 (at the end of a protest by the unemployed, which saw three bakeries looted) while attempting to prevent the police from interrogating Louise Michel. He was sentenced to prison for "armed looting." In 1889, he started publishing the famous tract, *Le Père peinard*. Taking asylum in England in 1894, he returned to France the following year, influenced by what he had seen of the English workers' struggle. He was a coauthor of the resolution since known as the *Charter of Amiens*, adopted at the 9th Congress of the *Confédération générale du travail* (CGT—General Confederation of Labor). The charter set out two aims for the union movement: daily demands; and the abolition of the salary system, independently of the state and political parties. It also advocated direct action and sabotage as means of struggle toward a general strike.

SPAIN

Buenaventura Durruti (1896–1936) was a militant Spanish worker and member of the *Confederación Nacional del Trabajo* (CNT—National Confederation of Labor). He defended the workers against the army and the bosses' private militias. During the Spanish Civil War, he led the famous Durruti Column on the Aragon front. He and his soldiers waged "war and revolution at the same time" in an army without military hierarchy, practicing self-discipline. This anarchist army abolished the salute, made pay equal, promoted a free press (for the newspapers at the front), encouraged free discussion, and convened battalion councils.

During fighting in the siege of Madrid, Durruti was struck by a mysterious stray bullet and died on November 10, 1936. The theory that it was a murder committed or ordered by the Communist Party has never been ruled out.

Leo Tolstoy (1828–1910) developed a religious anarchism in Russia, which had considerable influence in his time. This idea may be startling, but the thinking of Tolstoy, who rejected all recourse to violence, was strongly colored by anarchism. He was especially influenced by Proudhon, whom he met in 1862 (and from whom he took the title of his novel, *War and Peace*), as well as Kropotkin, with whom he corresponded. Like them, and with just as much fervor, Tolstoy was antistatist: "All government is an unsound institution, sanctified by custom and tradition to accomplish by force and total impunity the most revolting crimes." Like them, he envisaged an anarchist social order. This he refused to define in any detail because he believed that such a social organization would be achieved through a moral transformation rather than a political revolution. In his opinion, such a social organization would realize the meaning and significance of true Christianity, properly understood: Christians' rule of love and anarchists' stateless society tended in a similar direction. Tolstoy put nonviolence and the refusal to obey and collaborate with power at the heart of this program and moral revolution. Gandhi was the most famous of

Tolstoy's disciples. Tolstoy also inspired pacifists as well as more specifically religious groupings.

Tolstoy's offering of the reconciliation of Christian ideals (or religious ideals in general) alongside anarchist ideals had its later proponents. André Malraux had no doubts about it, writing, "Christ? An anarchist. The only one who succeeded."

Noam Chomsky

Noam Chomsky (1928–) is the best-known contemporary anarchist and among the most famous living intellectuals. For more than forty years, he has pursued two trajectories in his work: first, linguistics, a discipline that he greatly transformed and established scientifically; and second, political activism and criticism within the anarchist tradition, which he developed and renewed. Chomsky has always insisted on the independence of these two aspects of his work, claiming that only tenuous links can be drawn between them. It is as much a mistake to think that his linguistics theories are anarchist as it is to believe that his anarchism was inspired by or can in some way be deduced from his study of language.

Noam Chomsky was born in 1928 in Philadelphia. In 1957, he published *Syntactic Structures*, a major work that marked the beginning of what is known as the "Chomskyian revolution." Structuralism and behavioralism dominated linguistics at the time. Chomsky countered with the idea of a generative grammar, based on the potent and suggestive hypothesis of an innate language ability. In simple terms, children do not learn to speak, they know how to speak. Taking into account the knowledge of the locutors and of their creativity, understood as the capacity to produce and understand new and original utterances, Chomsky conceives of linguistics as tracing the transformations that link the underlying structure with the superficial structure of utterances in a given language. Concerned with a new object, the ability of the locutor, Chomsky's linguistics proves a particularly rich and fruitful way of studying and understanding the human mind. Even a simple overview of the diverse research projects undertaken by Chomsky since the 1950s would go far beyond the scope of this book. Here we will only note that, since 1966 in his *Cartesian Linguistics*, Chomsky has situated his work within the Cartesian rationalist tradition, drawing on its valuable epistemological teachings.

Chomsky's linguistics work has had a decisive influence extending far beyond his field to reach philosophy, psychology, and, more generally, all cognitive sciences.

Chomsky is, however, just as well known for his political contributions. During his adolescence, he frequented anarchist circles in New York, an experience which marked him indelibly; it would be truer to say that the dissident accidentally became a linguist rather than that the linguist became a dissident. In any case, Chomsky first came to prominence in the 1960s because of his opposition to the Vietnam War. He has since continued, vigilantly and forcefully, to provide a profound critique of American foreign policy, and his political work has continued to expand and have a great impact through present day.

Since I have already outlined how Chomsky conceives of anarchism and its historical development, we can immediately turn to the main elements of his work and contributions.

According to Chomsky, here influenced by Rudolf Rocker

(1873–1958), the development of modern capitalism has witnessed the progressive invasion and control of all political, economic, and ideological systems by what he calls "the vast institutions of private tyranny." Businesses, transnationals, banks, and other monetary and financial systems currently constitute the most developed and disturbing of these institutions of private tyranny. They are constructed hierarchically and have progressively freed themselves from all democratic control. According to Chomsky, they spring from the same soil as fascism and bolshevism, two other contemporary forms of totalitarianism. Spreading their influence in all directions, they engage in intense propaganda. Chomsky's work as an anarchist consists of tracking these structures, analyzing their actions, exposing their illegitimacy, and inviting people to fight them. His extremely rich, critical work makes Chomsky one of the most valuable observers in the world today. From the United States' imperialist machinations and free trade agreements, to transnationals and organizations like the International Monetary Fund and the World Bank, few aspects of international economics and politics in the past forty years have escaped his critical eye.

Democracies heavily rely on nonviolent methods to control thinking. For this reason, Chomsky is intensely interested in the role the media play in building consensus in contemporary societies. Closely examining these current forms of propaganda, he attempts to uncover the mechanisms of thought control and suggest possibilities for resistance. [See page 113.]

Elections: Suckers' Bait

Oh good elector, inexpressible imbecile, poor wretch . . . go home and start a strike.

——OCTAVE MIRBEAU

While agreeing with Bakunin that "the worst republic is a thousand times better than the most enlightened monarchy," anarchists have generally practiced abstention and have no words too harsh for the electoral lie of democracies. According to Élisée Reclus, "to vote is to abdicate." Albert Libertad denounced the voter as a "criminal" responsible for his own misfortunes: "Why do you bow, obey, serve? Why are you inferior, humiliated, offended, servant, slave? Because you are the voter, he who accepts what is; he who sanctions all his suffering, consecrates his own servitude through the ballot. You are the voluntary valet, the lovable domestic, the lackey, the flunky, the dog licking the whip. You are the jailer and the snitch. You are the good soldier, the willing tenant. You are the faithful employee, the devoted servant, the worker resigned to his own slavery. You are your own executioner. What are you complaining about?"

This position is often very much misunderstood. For anarchists, to vote is to choose one's own master and thus implicitly recognize that master's right to exist. To vote is to sanction one of the privileged ways in which the institutions and structures of power maintain themselves. To vote is to participate in a degrading and morally odious hoax that necessarily leads to lies, duplicity, and trickery, and guarantees that voters will be betrayed and duped. In the end, above all, to vote is to accept the practice of delegating and abdicating one's power.

The flip side of anarchists' refusal to vote is positive, however, and gives meaning to the abstentionist position: in their institutions and organizations, they attempt to practice direct democracy. In their view, this is the only form of democracy that is of value. This is also why anarchists always advocate direct action; that is, all forms of action in which people refuse to delegate their power, but act by and for themselves. Strikes, boycotts, occupations, sit-ins, sabotage, refusal to pay taxes, and roadblocks are a few examples. In Emma Goldman's words, the practice of direct action is "the favored method, logical and consistent with anarchism."

3. FACTS AND PLACES

Anarchism cannot be defined only in reference to a few theorists. It is also revealed through its history: one of uprisings, struggles, revolts, and revolutions in which anarchists took part alongside thousands of others.

Many high points mark this journey, as anarchism continued to clarify, correct, and refine itself. I would now like to briefly retrace this history, recalling some of the principal moments of anarchism.

The selection that follows is very limited. For the most part, it pertains to events in Europe and the Americas, excluding the many manifestations of anarchism in other continents. Moreover, it focuses on events that have had a certain historical impact. This is not to lose sight of the fact that direct action, mutual aid, solidarity, and the struggle against authority and for freedom and equality appear in all places and times and can often be found under the shadow of the state and all other forms of authority.

The International Workingmen's Association (1864–1876) and the Paris Commune (1871)

In the mid-nineteenth century, a significant movement to organize workers began. This movement became multifaceted and diverse, including many tendencies and factions, that were sometimes in opposition to each other. In the context of the accelerated industrialization of the nineteenth century, the decline of guilds, like the decline of brotherhoods of masters, first led to the Luddite movement. This workers' movement lashed out at the machines destroying the workers' way of life and their communities: what was sold to workers as progress meant a lowering of the quality of manufactured goods that, in their eyes, only profited capitalists and their collaborators.

Marx drew from this that there was a need for "time and experience before the workers, having learned to distinguish between machines and the capitalist use of them, direct their attacks not against production equipment but its social mode of exploitation." This is precisely the distinction that was made in the mid-nineteenth century, and the International Workingmen's Association marked an important moment in the history of the workers' movement.

Called the First International, it was born in London on September 28, 1864. The ideas and disciples of Marx—who had established the Communist League two decades earlier under the Manifesto of the Communist Party (1848)—were certainly present. Also present in force, however, were the Proudhonians. In fact, the statutes of the International, adopted at the Geneva Congress in 1866, were largely due to the work of a Parisian worker and disciple of Proudhon,

Henri-Louis Tolain (1828–1897). This text opens with a statement that "the emancipation of the workers must be the work of the workers themselves" and that "workers' efforts to achieve their emancipation must not lead to the constitution of new privileges, but should establish the same rights and same duties for everyone." However, the influence of the Proudhonians in the International dwindled and the faction led by Marx gained the upper hand at the Brussels Congress (1868). The debate that put the two currents at odds revolved chiefly around the question of property.

The Proudhonians did not succeed in convincing others of their distinction between property and possession. Tolain explained the distinction as follows: "Man has the right to appropriate everything he produces and to transform all rental contracts into sales contracts: so property, being constantly in circulation, ceases to be abusive by this very fact. Consequently, in agriculture and in industry, all workers will come together how and when it seems convenient, under the guarantee of a freely decided contract, safeguarding the freedom of individuals and groups." The contrary position, which Marx advanced, convinced the International to adopt the necessity of collectivization. A second wave of opposition soon emerged, this time brought forward by collectivist anarchists. Now the debate turned around the mode of organizing both the International and future society, and the means of getting there. These anarchists—James Guillaume and César de Paepe, in particular—were in favor of a federalist organization, a free union of free associations. They were opposed to centralization and, more strongly still, to the authoritarianism they perceived in their adversaries. Soon there was open talk of two factions within the International: the antiau-thoritarian communists and the authoritarian commu-nists. The latter were led by Marx and the former clustered around Bakunin, who had rejoined the International in 1868. The conflict between the two men was epic. It was a struggle not only between two doctrines, but also between two personalities.

Leaving aside the anecdotes, the drama, and the per-sonalities of the protagonists, however, the core debate was about authority. In 1872, at the Hague Congress, Marx had Bakunin expelled from the International. It was then decided to transfer the organization to the United States, but it was already moribund and dissolved in 1876.

In an article published in October 1872 in *La Liberté de Bruxelles*, Bakunin reflected on his conflict with Marx and the authoritarians. I have already quoted his remarkable prediction about the inevitability of a red bureaucracy in the wake of an authoritarian revolution establishing the "dictatorship of the proletariat." I will now reproduce an extract from the text in which Bakunin laid out the reasons for his opposition to the authoritarians and outlined the thinking on which this prediction was based:

> A state, a government, a universal dictatorship! The dream of Gregory VII, Boniface VIII, Charles XV and Napoleon is revived in a new form but with the same pretentions in the social democratic camp! . . . The Marxists . . . are devotees of state power, . . . champions of the established top-down order, always in the name of universal suffrage and

sovereignty of the masses, for whom is maintained the happiness and honor of obeying the leaders, the elected masters. . . . They accept no emancipation other than what they expect from their so-called people's state. . . . Marx dares to dream of subjecting the proletariat of all countries to a conformity of thought hatched in his own brain.

We can note that similar ideas were previously launched by Proudhon, who had also sharply denounced the "aggravated statism" of the communists and the "despotism" to which it led. Proudhon insisted that no one could bring about the revolution and that it would certainly not happen "on the command of a master with his preset theory or the prescription of a visionary."

The previous year, the Paris Commune (1871) had offered an opportunity for these two visions and these two conceptions of politics, revolution, and of the role of the state, to be put to the test. This spontaneous revolt established a free commune that sought to promote federalism and advocated contractual relations. Bakunin saw it as "the first obvious and practical manifestation" of anarchism. However, its failure had in effect already been declared by Proudhon, who remarked, "What use is it if Paris has revolutions within the confines of its walls! If Lyons, Marseilles, Toulouse, Bordeaux, Nantes, Rouen, Lille, Strasbourg, Dijon, etc., if the independent townships don't follow, the hopes of Paris will be frustrated."

The defeat of the Commune nevertheless held rich and valuable lessons for the anarchists. The Commune, they believed, had not gone far enough in the direction of decentralization. It had not completed the process of destroying the state within itself. It had not pushed economic reforms to the point of self-organization. It had not arrived at authentic and complete participatory democracy. Finally, it had failed to complete its political and economic revolutions with a social revolution. In this way, Kropotkin wrote that the Communards had tried to consolidate the Commune first, postponing the social revolution until later, while "the only possible way was to consolidate the Commune through social revolution." It is remarkable that, at first, Marx drew libertarian lessons from the Commune, in the end very close to Bakunin's position (*La Guerre civile en France*, 1871). Only later did he adopt the orthodox position that communists have since held, which posits the necessity of a revolutionary state, the importance of the phase of the "dictatorship of the proletariat" and, among other dogmas, the central place of the Party.

In 1872, in Saint-Imier, anarchists founded their own International Federation, notably uniting the Spanish, Italian, and Jurassian federations. In Spain, anarchism would soon be particularly alive, present, and active; this intensity preceded the CNT's, founded at the beginning of the next century—we'll come back to it in the context of the Spanish Civil War.

The Italian Federation, heavily influenced by Bakunin, was also active and important. The Jurassian Federation was shared by followers of Proudhon and Bakunin. After 1880, the anarchist movement adopted, with increasing unanimity, the anarcho-communist positions of Kropotkin. At this time, anarchists were focusing a great deal of discussion and analysis on elaborating the society they envisaged, in an attempt to demonstrate its desirability and to prove that it was not utopic.

In 1877, the events of Benevento in which Malatesta participated inaugurated the practice of "propaganda by the deed." In an April 1880 issue of *Le Révolté*, Kropotkin called it "a permanent revolt by speech, writing, dagger, rifle, dynamite. . . . Everything is good for us which is outside legality." It was a dark period in the history of anarchism. This practice culminated in France between 1892 and 1894 before rapidly spreading to diverse countries, always with the same disastrous results.

The origin of this movement has been identified as a meeting between Bakunin and a young Russian nihilist, Sergey Nechayev, who came to seek approval and legitimacy from the famous revolutionary. At this time, anarchists were progressively isolated in the workers' movements and especially in the First International. Out of a kind of bitterness, they adopted "propaganda of the deed" as their byword, first at the Bern Congress (1876) and then again at the Saint-Imier Congress (1877). It was supposed to replace spoken or written propaganda, now deemed to be ineffective. The "chimeric and adventurist virus," as Daniel Guérin put it, was thus introduced into the movement. "Propaganda by the deed" most often took the form of attacks against high-profile political figures. According to Henri Arvon, these attacks were expected to "strike the imagination of the people through terror" and thus "pull the masses out of their apathy."

The goal would never be achieved through these means, as Kropotkin soon recognized: "A structure founded on centuries of history cannot be destroyed by a few kilos of explosives." This episode led to strange phenomena, not the least of which was that a substantial part of the population, as well as otherwise respectable artists and intellectuals, made heroes or martyrs of sometimes debatable individuals, who were nevertheless victims of bourgeois justice and public condemnation.

The assassination of French president Sadi Carnot in 1894 led to the introduction of repressive laws citing "press infractions." Baptized "rogue laws" by those who rightly saw them as a major violation of press freedom, they brought an end to the years of "propaganda by the deed" in France. However, in many other countries, revolutionaries continued the practice, assassinating political figures such as Empress Elizabeth of Austria in 1898, King Umberto (or Humbert) I in 1900, and William McKinley, president of the United States, 1901. The next event marking the history of anarchism took place in the latter country, in Chicago.

Haymarket Massacre (1886)

The anarchist origins and meaning of May 1st have long since been forgotten. This date in fact marks a major event in the history of the workers' movement and, more specifically, of anarchism, although we commemorate it without knowing its original meaning. Let's go back in time. We are in 1886, in Chicago. In this city, as in the entire country, the workers' movement is vibrant, lively, and active. In Chicago, the anarchists are firmly established. Anarchist daily newspapers are published in the various languages of the immigrant communities. The most famous of these, the *Arbeiter Zeitung*, prints more than 25,000 copies this year, while the workers' movement is engaged in a fight for the eight-hour day. The anarchists are involved, but with their usual lucidity: the eight-hour day for now, certainly, but without losing sight of the real goal, the complete abolition of the salary system. Under these circumstances, the general strike of May 1, 1886, was broadly respected, especially in Chicago. August Spies, a well-known anarchist activist in the Windy City, was one of the last to speak to the impressive crowd of protestors. As the crowd dispersed, the protest, calm and peaceful up to that point, took a dramatic turn: two hundred police officers suddenly charged the workers. There was one death, and dozens were injured. Spies went straight to the *Arbeiter Zeitung* and wrote a call to protest against the police violence. This protest took place on May 4 in Haymarket Square in Chicago. Once again, it began calmly. August Spies spoke, as did two other anarchists, Albert Parsons and Samuel Fielden.

The mayor of Chicago, Carter Harrison, attended the protest and as it unfolded became convinced that nothing would happen. He advised the police chief, Inspector John Bonfield, of this and asked him to send home the police officers stationed nearby. It was 10:00 p.m. and raining heavily. Fielden finished his speech, the last one scheduled. The protestors were dispersing and only a few hundred remained in Haymarket Square. Suddenly, 180 police officers appeared and rushed towards the crowd. Fielden protested. A bomb was thrown at the police. It killed one and wounded dozens. The police opened fire on the crowd, killing unknown numbers of people.

A witchhunt was launched throughout the city. The authorities demanded the guilty. Seven anarchists were arrested: August Spies, Samuel Fielden, Adolph Fischer,

George Engel, Michael Schwab, Louis Lingg, and Oscar Neebe. An eighth was added when Albert Parsons turned himself in, convinced that he couldn't be convicted of anything because he was innocent, like the others. In fact, only three of the eight suspects were even present at Haymarket on the fatal evening of May 4.

The trial of the eight began on June 21, 1886, at the Cook County Criminal Court. It could not, and cannot, be proven that any of them had thrown the bomb, were connected with the person responsible for the act, or had even approved of it.

From the outset it was evident to everyone that this was a trial not so much of these men but of the workers' movement in general, and of anarchism in particular. The jury selection became farcical, in the end, uniting people who shared a hatred of anarchists. It even included a relative of one of the police officers who had been killed. Judge Joseph Gary was no worse than the prosecutor, Julius Grinnell, who declared in his instructions to the jury, "The republic is just a step away from anarchy. The law itself is on trial. Anarchy is on trial. These eight men have been selected because they are leaders. They are no more guilty than the thousands who follow them. Gentlemen of the jury; convict these men, make examples of them, hang them and you save our institutions, our society." On August 19, all were sentenced to death except Oscar Neebe, who was slammed with fifteen years in prison. The trial had been so patently absurd that the sentences provoked a huge international protest movement. It succeeded in getting Michael Schwab's and Samuel Fielden's sentences commuted to life in prison. Lingg hanged himself in his cell.

Parsons, Engel, Spies, and Fischer were hung on November 11, 1887. History refers to them as the "Haymarket Martyrs." More than half a million people turned out for their funerals. May 1 was declared a day of commemoration so that these events would not be forgotten. Neebe, Schwab, and Fielden were officially freed on June 26, 1893; they were declared innocent, and the fact that they had been the victims of a campaign of hysteria and a biased trial was recognized. The intention of those responsible for convicting the Chicago martyrs remains clear: to break the workers' movement and destroy the anarchist movement in the United States. The same day that the death sentence was pronounced on the four anarchists, Chicago slaughterhouse workers were informed that they would return to ten-hour workdays the following Monday.

After the 1890s, having progressively abandoned "propaganda of the deed," anarchists returned to other means: education [see page 104], the press, cooperative projects, and then syndicalism, which was a rich and significant experience [see page 107].

The anarchist spirit reemerged in Germany with the transformation of the Free Association of German Unions, which combined with a local entity into an anarcho-syndicalist organization, the *Freie Arbeiter-Union Deutschlands* (FAUD—Free Workers' Union of Germany) in 1919, and then the creation of the International Workers' Association (IWA) in 1922 in Berlin. The IWA brought together anarcho-syndicalist organizations from thirty European and American countries—including the CNT in Spain, USI in Italy, CGT in Portugal, SAC in Sweden, and FORA in Argentina—representing more than two million unionized workers. The first secretariat included Rudolf Rocker, Augustin Souchy, and Alexander Schapiro. Again in Germany, the Union of Workers (AAUD) formed following a schism in the German Workers Communist Party (KAPD) in 1921. The AAUD partook of the anarchist spirit to the extent that its members wanted to abolish the distinction—central to social democracy and then to Leninism—between political action and the economic struggle. They also rejected traditional organizing forms; in the words of council communist Otto Rühe, their philosopher, they believed that "the revolution isn't a party affair."

When the factories were occupied during Red Week in Italy, it was possible to believe, for a brief moment, that a social revolution would erupt. This hope was short-lived. It was overtaken by the First World War and the Manifesto of the Sixteen, which provoked a split and bitter debates within the movement.

With this retreat, one can only be grateful to those activists who resisted war-mongering and patriotic jingoism, countering it with the pacifism and internationalism that anarchists had always advocated. Sébastien Faure and Louis Lecoin were among these. The letter that Lecoin sent from prison to the military leader of Paris on September 12, 1918, is well known. It reads in part, "I firmly believe that a man can and must refuse to kill another. War fomented by global capitalism is the most horrible of crimes. I am protesting it by not responding to the mobilization order. By refusing to obey the rule of the soldier, by refusing to allow myself to be militarized, I am acting according to my anarchist ideals."

The Russian Revolution presented anarchists with a vast new challenge.

The Russian Revolution (1917–1921)

The Russian Revolution was a major event of the twentieth century and has thus been intensely studied. We tend to believe that we know all about it. However, an understanding of the role that anarchists played in the affair provides an unusual perspective, offering a glimpse into what Vsevolod Voline (1882–1945) called the "unknown revolution." This has been almost entirely obscured by official history, beginning with the one written by the Communists.

The Revolution that took place in Russia in October 1917 was rooted in the popular revolts of 1905 and specifically in the workers' councils—called Soviets—that emerged at that time. Trotsky made no mistake: "The Soviet's activity signified the organization of anarchy." The terrain for October had also been prepared by the revolution of February 1917, which overthrew tsarism and installed a faltering and divided power. Returning from exile, Lenin promulgated his April Theses. He opposed the war, but, with the opportunism he never failed to practice, called for "All power to the Soviets." This idea was too radical to be well received by the Bolshevik party. It was, however, necessary. From the beginning of what became the October Revolution, the Russian people had revived the Soviets, previously initiated in 1905. They were omnipresent and the Bolsheviks had no choice but to accommodate them. As most historians now recognize, the Bolsheviks seized power on October 25, 1917, in what was essentially a coup d'état by a minority group, without real popular support. Key to the success of the Bolsheviks was their skill in maneuvering in the context of great social disorder, further aggravated by war, and their policy of making promises which followed the aspirations of the majority. In other words, the Bolsheviks were opportunists who succeeded in hijacking a huge, autonomous social movement. This opportunism was not slow to show itself in their policies.

At the beginning of 1918, a separate peace was negotiated with Germany and Austria. The measures adopted were very popular. Lenin presented them as a way for "anarchist ideas" to assume "living forms." The Bolsheviks recognized ownership of land by the peasants and ownership of factories by the workers; they nationalized businesses and banks, and launched the slogan, "All power to the Soviets." This convinced the Russian anarchists to support the government, which seemed to offer the best hope for the revolution. Some even decided to participate. Very quickly, however—in fact, as soon as these concessions allowed them to assumed control over the revolution—the Bolsheviks reverted to their authoritarian ideas and practices. It should be remembered that the war was not yet over and was aggravated in Russia by foreign intervention. The weakened economy and civil society were disorganized. Seizing this pretext, the Bolsheviks outlawed all other parties and established their "dictatorship of the proletariat." Arbitrary arrests and executions began. Anarchists were among the first targeted. By the spring of 1918, the Soviets were finished, systematically eliminated by the Bolsheviks in just a few months. The unions—and soon, all forms of free, grassroots organization—followed. Statements by the Bolshevik leaders left no doubt about their intentions. Lenin explained that a large-scale industrial economy, in his view, required an "absolute and strict unity of purpose," which could only be ensured by the complete submission of the "multitude to a single purpose." He continued, "All authority, in a factory, must therefore be concentrated in the hands of the management, and that being the case, any direct intervention by unions in the management of businesses must be viewed as positively harmful and unacceptable." And more specifically, "A producers' congress? What exactly is that supposed to mean? It is difficult to find words to describe such foolishness. I keep asking myself if it is a farce. How can one take such people seriously? While production is always necessary, democracy is not."

Voline had already responded, "The incompetence of the masses. What a fabulous tool for exploiters and oppressors past, present and to come and particularly for our current aspiring slave-drivers, whatever their denomination— Nazism, Bolshevism, Fascism, Communism. Incompetence of the masses: this is where reactionaries of all colors are in perfect agreement with the Communists. And this agreement is highly significant."

From 1918 to 1920, civil war destroyed the country. Famine and epidemics led to the death of millions. The Tenth Congress of 1921 adopted the New Economic Policy (NEP) and at the same time forbade all allegiances that had been purged from the party. The revolution was finished, the socialist episode definitively over. Starting in 1922, Russia's imperial region was reconstituted as the Union of Soviet Socialist Republics (USSR), a new currency was created and the country opened to foreign capital. In the same year, Lenin created the post of secretary-general of the party for Joseph Stalin. Two other events marked the obliteration of anarchist ideals and the USSR's shift towards authoritarianism and totalitarianism: the crushing of Makhnovtchina, between 1919 and 1921 in the Ukraine; and the Kronstadt rebellion in March 1921. The Makhnovstchina borrowed its name from a young Ukrainian anarchist peasant, Nestor Makhno (1888–1934). In 1917, Makhno was released from prison, where he had spent long years and received the only education he would ever get. First, he waged guerrilla warfare against the German and Austrian armies of occupation, showing remarkable talent as a tactician. His army, whose internal organization prefigured the Durruti Column, proved particularly effective. In the areas in which they operated, Makhno and his troops encouraged and, for the first time on this scale, enabled the establishment of an authentically anarchist society. Daniel Guérin cites a poster the Makhnovists put up in the areas they entered: "The freedom of the peasants and workers belongs to themselves alone and can suffer no restriction. It is up to the peasants and workers themselves to act, organize, come to agreement. . . . The makhnovists can only help them, giving some advice or suggestions. . . . But in no case can they—nor do they want to—govern them."

After the armistice, Makhno then fought the counter-revolutionary White Army led by General Anton Denikin, but his relations with the Bolsheviks rapidly deteriorated. He refused to put his army under the command of Trotsky, who liquidated the Makhnovtchina after long months of fighting, which ended in August 1921. Exiled, Makhno lived out the rest of his life in Paris. He documented his own story; Voline and Peter Arshinov did as well, and Durruti was able to learn from his combat experience.

The memory of Makhno and the Makhnovtchina is still very much alive in the Ukraine. The Kronstadt rebellion is another powerful symbol of how the Bolsheviks physically eliminated their rivals in order to gain control over popular revolts.

Kronstadt was a naval base on an island in the Gulf of Finland, not far from Petrograd. Its sailors had already played an important role in the events of 1905. They had also played an active, even crucial, role in the initial stages of the October Revolution, notably by blocking Lavr Kornilov's counterrevolutionary putsch in August 1917, and by providing frontline defense of Petrograd. But their action, based on defense of the revolution and the Soviets, soon brought them into hostilities with the Bolsheviks, once the latter dropped their pretense of supporting the Soviets. The inevitable happened a few days after the Tenth Congress of the Russian Communist Party began.

The Kronstandt sailors rose up, and on March 1 they made a series of demands: election of soviets by universal and secret ballot; freedom of speech, press, meeting, and association; creation of free unions; freedom for political prisoners; abolition of party privilege and the dissolution of its armed wings; free access to land for peasants; and the right to exist of small manufacturers operating on wage systems.

These proposals were obviously unacceptable to the Bolsheviks. The reprisals weren't long in coming. Trotsky threatened to "bomb them like sitting ducks." On March 7, 1921, the sailors issued a famous tract, "Everyone knows!," which threatened, "The blood of innocents will rebound on the heads of the communists, maddened fools intoxicated by power." Sometime previously, Kropotkin had offered the same evaluation, in similar terms: "Lenin is not comparable to any other revolutionary figure in history. Revolutionaries have ideals. Lenin has none. He's a madman, a high priest of sacrifice, desirous of burning, massacring, and sacrificing. Good and evil have no meaning for him. He is willing to betray all of Russia to carry out an experiment."

On March 18, the Kronstadt rebellion ended in a bloodbath. Emma Goldman wrote that, for her, as for many other anarchist observers, this event had destroyed "the last vestiges of the Bolshevik myth."

Voline's comment is well known. He observed that the main lesson of the Russian Revolution was "how not to do a revolution" and that, in every way, it fulfilled Bakunin's prophecy about the emergence of a red bureaucracy and a monstrous dictatorship.

Anarchists worldwide at first observed events unfolding in Russia with enthusiasm. As news about what was really happening began to reach them, their enthusiasm waned, finally giving way to a total condemnation of Bolshevism. This assessment has never been revised.

For very different reasons, both market and planned economies had stakes in calling this bloody experiment "socialism" and "communism." Neither has revised this position.

The First World War and the Russian Revolution together dealt a heavy blow to the anarchist movement, but their activities continued. Journals and periodicals continued to appear, congresses were held, and books were published. The movement even expanded somewhat in Latin America (especially in Argentina, but also Peru and Chile), as well as Mexico and Cuba. Factory occupations, quickly stifled, took place in Italy in August and September 1920. Their defeat was followed by the terrible ordeal of fascism, a preventive counterrevolution. The real bastion of anarchism in the interwar period then became Spain. Here anarchism underwent its great historical experiment and entered into conflict with the forces of fascism, capitalism, and Stalinism, all which combined to crush it.

The Spanish Civil War (1936–1939)

Much has been written about the Spanish Civil War. It should be acknowledged that a substantial part of this literature is based on propaganda and falsification from all sides. However, sixty years after these terrible events, there is general agreement on key aspects, allowing for an understanding of the origins and unfolding of the war, as well as the part played by anarchists.

First a few facts indispensable to understanding all of the complexities of these events: In 1936, Spain, still suffering the severe effects of the 1929 economic crisis, was a largely agrarian country struggling through a process of industrialization. Some 675,000 of the 80 million inhabitants were unemployed. The country was troubled by numerous and very deep political, ideological, and economic conflicts. Its oligarchy hobnobbed with a powerful church and could rely on the support of a large army that had an appetite for *pronunciamientos* (military coups d'état).

On the other side were grassroots and labor movements predominantly influenced by anarchism. Unlike elsewhere, where authoritarian communist or reformist social-democratic tenets and parties ultimately prevailed, the Spanish labor movement was still shaped by the ideas and practices of Bakunin and anarcho-syndicalism. The large-scale anarchist experiment occasioned by the Spanish Civil War had thus been long in preparation. In 1936, the anarcho-syndicalist CNT was the largest union in Spain. It had more than a million and a half members, and its spirit and driving force was the *Federacion anarquista Iberica* (FAI) (Iberian Anarchist Federation).

The elections of February 18, 1936, brought in a leftist coalition, the *Frente Popular*. Three factors helped bring about this victory. First, the agrarian reforms undertaken by the previous government failed; second, the leftist coalition promised a political amnesty; and finally, though no less significantly, the anarchists launched a call to vote for the *Frente Popular* (although, as we might guess, they did not participate in the coalition). In sum, Spain was divided into two irreconcilably opposed camps, with conflicts crystallizing along the dividing line: on one side, a left that included republicans, socialists, communists, and anarchists; on the other, a right consisting of oligarchs, Carlists, royalists, Catholics, and the Falange of José Antonio Primo de Rivera, with the backing of a mighty and loyal army.

The government began to implement its program in a troubled, tense context. On June 16, the monarchist leader Jose Calvo Sotelo delivered a famous speech: "Against this sterile state, I propose the integral state. Many will call it fascist. But if the fascist state means an end to strikes, an end to disorder, an end to property abuse, then I am proud to call myself a fascist. I count any soldier crazy who is not prepared before eternity to stand up to anarchy if it is necessary."

The situation became extremely tense when Sotelo was

assassinated on July 13. His death triggered *el alzamiento* on July 17 in Melilla—a military uprising that had been in preparation for some weeks. Francisco Franco left the Canary Islands and assumed command of the troops from Morocco. The workers' militias mounted a heroic resistance and, against all expectation, the coup d'état did not succeed as the military had planned. Spain was cut in two. Madrid, Barcelona, and Valencia remained under republican control, along with the entire Mediterranean coast. For almost three years, two zones, two regimes, two ideologies confronted each other in bloody battles, in which heightened emotions encouraged recourse to summary justice. The Italian Fascist and German Nazi regimes provided substantial aid to the franquists, while the democracies abandoned Spain by adopting a shameful neutrality. Stalinist USSR supported the republicans. Two series of events unfolded: a classic civil war in which fascists opposed republicans; and, within republican territory, a profound anarchist social revolution.

The war ended on March 29, 1939. It had lasted thirty-two months, with one million deaths. It left the country in ruins.

More than sixty thousand volunteers joined the famous international brigades, as well as the CNT militias (international group of the Durruti Column) and the *Partido Obrero de Unificacion Marxista* (POUM) (Worker's Party of Marxist Unification), an anti-Stalinist communist party.

Now let's turn to the anarchist social revolution, its most notable achievements, and the factors that contributed to its failure.

Everything had been long prepared: minds and practice,

books, newspapers, periodicals, discussions, schools, and experiments of all kinds. The CNT's mode of operating, especially its *sindicatos unitos* (union locals), provided direct experience for many passionate debates on the organization of free communes of the future. In May 1936, the anarchists gathered at the Saragossa congress had already adopted an ambitious, altruistic model of an anarchist commune, detailing the workings of their concept of direct democracy, highlighting the importance they ascribed to cultivating intellect, and outlining potential means of establishing such communes. The ideas of Diego Abad de Santillan also had considerable impact. De Santillan had just published *After the Revolution*, a real *aggiornamento* of anarchist positions on the economy.

The beginning of the war and the armed popular uprising against the military putsch offered the Spanish anarchists all they had hoped for in a spontaneous revolt.

In the republican zone, things happened very quickly and mostly outside the influence of the state, which had become largely superfluous. The elites fled, leaving behind factories and unoccupied lands, which were rapidly collectivized. Workers and peasants began putting anarchism into practice and implementing its apolitical program. Their attitude to politicians was exactly as described by Daniel Guérin: do as you will, we will take over the economy, prelude and condition for stifling the state.

Again quoting Guérin, these far-reaching experiments in self-organization, accompanied by spectacular social transformations, are "the most positive legacy of Spanish anarchism." According to Gaston Leval, eight million people participated in these, directly or indirectly. The collectivization was agrarian, of course, but it was also industrial, and in some regions, it soon affected all aspects of collective life.

Sam Dolgoff summarized that these collectives worked

without owners, without bosses, and without capitalist competition to stimulate production. In most industries, factories, mills, workshops, transportation services, and public services, the workers, their revolutionary committees, and their unions reorganized and managed production, distribution, and services without any highly paid management and without reference to state authority. . . . Their efforts were coordinated by free association across vast areas and enabled a growth in production (especially in agriculture), an increase in the number of schools, and an improvement in public services.

According to the best informed, *Revolution and War in Spain* by Pierre Broué and Émile Témime remains one of the best sources on the Spanish Civil War. The conclusion of their chapter on revolutionary gains is worth quoting in its entirety:

To assess the revolutionary achievements fairly, the terrible war burden must be taken into account. The revolutionary conquests of the Spanish workers had important and profoundly significant consequences in the first months. New management principles, the abolition of dividends allowed an effective decrease in prices. This was only reversed by the dizzying increase in costs of raw materials, which a capitalist economy would also have been unable to avoid in similar conditions. Mechanization and rationalization, introduced into numerous businesses on the demand of the workers themselves, considerably increased productivity. Workers enthusiastically agreed to enormous sacrifices because in most cases they were convinced that the factory belonged to them and that they were at last working for themselves and others in their class. A new spirit infused the Spanish economy; scattered industries were concentrated, commercial channels simplified, and a whole infrastructure of social achievements realized for old workers, children, invalids, the sick, and all working people. The weakness of the revolutionary gains of the Spanish workers lay not so much in their improvised nature as in the fact that they were incomplete. Because the revolution, barely born, had to defend itself. It was the war which reduced the revolutionary achievements to mere scraps before they had had the opportunity to ripen and be put to the test of daily experience—reverses and advances, experiments and discoveries.

Their last point raises the question of what caused the failure of the collectivizations and, more generally, of the anarchist revolution in Spain. The causes are complex, and a careful inquiry into this question is outside the scope of this book. However, we can at least note that, although

Pierre Broué and Emile Témime are obviously correct in assessing that the war played an important part in this failure, it was not the only factor. In addition to confronting the forces of Franco, Benito Mussolini, and Adolf Hitler, and with no support from the democracies, the revolution faced deep internal divisions. Eventually these led to the communists' seizing control over the course of events. Prior to that, the anarchists made—according to more than one commentator—an unpardonable and fatal error: participation in the government. They did so with the intention of prioritizing the struggle against fascism over the revolution and because they were convinced of the provisional and circumstantial neutrality of the state. From that point on, they were irrevocably enmeshed, and the authorities, which included some anarchists, undertook the destruction of the social revolution and collectives—in lockstep with the reconstruction of state apparatus.

The reformers, communists, and republican bourgeoisie found a ready-made ally in Stalin. From the beginning of the conflict, the communists had portrayed the events in Spain as a simple internal affair, without great importance. Complex geopolitical and ideological interests informed this stance. From the outset, the USSR denied the revolutionary nature of the events and continued to reassure real or potential allies against the Italo-German threat.

Against the gold reserves of the Bank of Spain, the USSR offered a modest amount of aid; as always, this remained under its management, the better to assume control over events at any moment. From the end of 1936, the Soviet press made no mystery of the USSR's goals in Spain: to reestablish a pluralist republican democracy and to right the "uncontrolled elements" of the CNT and the "POUM Trotskyists." (The defeat of the revolution in Spain left the USSR as the sole representative of a socialist society and its model of communism the only one on offer.)

In the spring of 1937, the republican state, no longer a democracy in any sense, expanded its repressive measures. In May, a bloody confrontation in Barcelona pitted anarchists and POUM members against the communists. The communist repression began a few days later. First came the arrest and conviction of the POUM leaders. Then, throughout the summer of 1937, a parallel police force created by Soviet and Spanish communists arrested, tortured, and imprisoned hundreds of anarchists, disbanded their committees, closed their spaces, pillaged the collectives, and reestablished the state and private property. In August, the Military Investigation Service was created, with prisons, concentration camps, and six thousand agents at its disposal, under the control of the Stalinists. The rest is history.

In May 1939, the Spanish fascists, surrounded by Mussolini's Black Shirts and troops from Hitler's Condor Legion—responsible for the Guernica massacre—marched into Madrid. (Three months later, they were in Warsaw.) They paraded in front of Franco, who had said he was ready to shoot half of Spain if necessary to get there. The Second World War was about to break out; for the main actors, the events in Spain constituted no more than a dress rehearsal heralding the horrors that would soon be unleashed on the world.

The memory of the Spanish Civil War remains bitter, and not only for anarchists. To feel that bitterness, it is enough to be a friend of freedom and democracy.

The failure of the Spanish revolution was devastating for the anarchist movement, which ceased assuming a lead role in social struggles. The movement and its history, ideas, and achievements nevertheless endured. A nucleus of anarchist activists and thinkers carried it forward, feeding and inspiring many.

And in 1968, despite those who had mothballed the old political ideas a little too hastily, anarchism reemerged.

The "Redoubtable Revolt of May" 1968

Between May 3 and June 16, 1968, most major cities in France were in a state of intense upheaval. The spirit was symbolized by *Les Enragés* and the Movement of March 22, when a hundred students occupied the Faculty of Literature of Paris University at Nanterre to protest the arrest of another student after a demonstration against the Vietnam War. The anarchist group and journal *Noir et Rouge* (*Black and Red*) played an influential role.

On May 3, the secretary-general of the French Communist Party, Georges Marchais, denounced the "German anarchist," Daniel Cohn-Bendit in *L'Humanité*.

Building on numerous radical social struggles since the beginning of the decade, May 1968 was launched. Students, then teachers, went on strike, erecting barricades, and holding many protests.

Factories were spontaneously occupied and then, jumping on the bandwagon, unions joined the movement, calling for a general strike. On May 20, seven million people were on strike throughout the country. However, the movement weakened as the institutional left co-opted and then diverted it. The clear hostility of the Communist Party played a major role. On May 30, a large protest led by the Gaullists marched down the Champs-Élysées. It was the beginning of the end of May 1968.

While the May movement featured many anarchist traits, the anarchist federations were not greatly involved (apart from the small groups named above). As Louis Mercier Vega wrote,

> [I]t's not the French Anarchist Federation that is putting its activists or its flags within the student movements; the students themselves are raising the black flag to symbolize their desire for a blank slate and to throw into question all hierarchies. And it is the students who, from jumbled memories of readings and the pantheon of archetypes, have assembled a past based on Bakunin, Bonnot, and Durruti.

Among the currents that best symbolize the anarchist inspiration on the margins of the official movement is the situationist movement. Guy Debord (1931–1994) and Raoul Vaneigem (1934) are the best known and most remarkable figures of situationism.

The *Internationale situationniste* (IS) magazine was founded in 1957. At that time, it was the mouthpiece of an avant-garde art movement, descended from Dada, Surrealism, and Letterism, devoted to radically challenging the concept of art and putting "imagination in power." However, influenced by the ideas generated by the group *Socialisme ou Barbarie* (Socialism or Barbarism), (which offered a radical critique of Soviet bureaucracy), and by the writings of Henri Lefebvre on everyday life (*Critique de la vie quoti-dienne* [*Critique of Everyday Life*], 1961), IS members soon rediscovered the idea of a different kind of socialism, most notably the power of workers' councils. Their analysis then began to stretch far beyond the sphere of culture and art. Hostile to the Communist Party and Soviet state capitalism and its bureaucracy, the situationists produced writings in the 1960s that should be remembered beyond the slogans that flourished on the walls of May 1968—"*L'imagination au pouvoir!*" (Power to the imagination!), of course, but also others, including, "*L'économie est blessée: qu'elle crève!*" (The economy is wounded: may it crash!); "*Soyez réaliste: demandez l'impossible*" (Be realistic: demand the impossible); and "*Vivre sans temps mort*" (Live without downtime)." The IS was much more than a reservoir of poetic slogans: it inspired and theorized May 1968, particularly through a remarkable book by Debord.

Debord published *Société du spectacle* (*The Society of the Spectacle*) in 1967, rightly calling it the "only theory of the redoubtable May revolt." The "spectacle," as a social relation, is presented by the author as the key to understanding contemporary forms of alienation, of defining the process of social mystification at work in our societies. The spectacle permanently produces a reified reality, imposing its images, appearances, and fictions, which force us to live through representation. Debord wrote, "In societies under the sway of modern conditions of production, all of life appears as a vast accumulation of spectacles. Direct experience is distanced by representation."

According to Debord, from this analysis grows a desire to reappropriate daily life; a desire to transform the perception of the world through spontaneous "deviation" and "celebration." This revolt, which the situationists believed they were catalyzing, would necessarily lead to an anarchist, self-organized society. This was May 1968: people seized on a lust for life, forms of direct democracy multiplying.

The Situationist International dissolved in 1972, but its ideas have continued to exercise an undeniable influence and to circulate within the ebb and flow of anarchist ideas. Guy Debord died in 1994. However, Raoul Vaneigem recently published a remarkable *Avertissement aux écoliers et lycéens* (*A Warning to Students of All Ages*), written in clearly anarchist terms. Moreover, books produced by the successors of the situationists' publishing house (Éditions Ivrea and the *Encyclopédie des nuisances*) carry the same vigorous critical thought.

Arts, Literature, Aesthetics

While anarchism certainly suffered stinging defeats in the social and political fields, it has never ceased to generate brilliant triumphs in the fields of art and literature.

—HENRI ARVON

Is there a properly anarchist art or literature? Is there an aesthetic—that is, a theory of art—to which either of these can lay claim? Some believe so and have attempted to demonstrate it. In my view, they have not been very convincing.

This is not terribly surprising. An art that is "anarchist" would, by definition, lose just about all that would be of interest. It would cease to be alive and innovative even as it submitted to the dictates in which it accepted to enclose itself. Many anarchists have been interested in art and have written about it, beginning with Proudhon and Kropotkin. While their writing on art is obscure (and, to be honest, of little interest to me), other anarchist reflections on art, such as Trotsky's *What is Art?*, are both well-known and of lasting interest. However, no aesthetic emerges from any of this that is specifically anarchist or that would allow the elaboration of anarchist positions on art theory questions such as the nature of beauty or the meaning of art.

However, ties between the world of art and literature and the world of anarchism have consistently been rich and fertile. A simple enumeration of all the writers, painters, and artists who have been inspired by anarchism—or were themselves anarchists—would fill all the space I have for this topic.

From Percy Bysshe Shelley, Gustave Courbet, Camille Pissarro, Henrik Ibsen, and Paul Signac to Marcel Duchamp (who called himself "anartist"), and from John Cage to the Surrealists, the list is impressive. The ties between anarchism and the art world were especially plentiful and rich at the end of the nineteenth century, with symbolism and Impressionism.

What is the explanation for this constant interplay? Artists are not oblivious to the place anarchism accords to freedom and individuality as well as revolt and emancipation from tradition.

For example, the painter Signac described his work as "a personal effort of one's entire individuality against the official bourgeois conventions." Their passion for freedom opened the eyes of anarchists to the great danger that any subjugation to the political posed for authentic art. For this reason, the use of art as propaganda, or any attempt to commandeer it for the defense or promotion of a political program, is very unusual within any of the anarchist currents. Far from wanting to regiment art, anarchism has preferred to emphasize the creative act over the creator, thereby avoiding personality cults and their attendant mythologies.

Anarchism rejected economic and historical reductionism, developed by the Marxist aesthetic to the point of caricature in socialist realism (of which Marx held a very dim view). Instead, it has always preferred to look to the future and the unknown.

4. POSITIONS

Anarchism takes positions on a wide variety of issues, some unique to anarchism and some shared with other currents of thought. This chapter introduces these positions: eight parts forming five more or less unified groupings.

The first grouping examines anarchist positions on *production*, understood in the broadest sense of the term. From the outset, anarchists devoted lengthy studies to the economy, production, and the consumption of goods. Their ideal of self-organization is still adopted by many activists. The example of participatory economies shows that it has not lost the power to feed reflection and inspire action [see page 92]. Historically, *anarcho-syndicalism* was one of the means anarchists favored to defend workers and to promote and realize the kind of society they advocated [see page 97]. Under the *ecological imperative* of our era, this awareness has served as a basis for anarchist reflection on new forms of the social organization of production [see page 101].

The second grouping begins by highlighting how anarchism's concern for the emancipation and freedom of all has led to devoting significant thought and effort to *education*. Still today, anarchism has many strong and original ideas to offer in this area [see page 104]. The *media* now play such an important role in shaping minds in our democracies. It is scarcely surprising that anarchists have focused on this system of indoctrination by analyzing the media and other means of controlling public opinion, particularly public relations firms [see page 113].

The third grouping examines anarchist values. Its morality indicates an anarchist *ethics* and meta-ethics that I will attempt to sketch [see page 118].

The fourth grouping is on *anarcho-feminism* [see page 123], and the fifth and last, *anarcho-capitalism* [see page 126]. The subject of intense debate, the currency of this latter issue is great and its importance undeniable. This justifies giving it a fair amount of space.

Economy

To briefly characterize its position on economics, anarchism has advocated self-organization since the nineteenth century, forcefully rejecting—and proposing the abolishment of—what it calls wage slavery, as intolerable in every way. In other words, anarchism demands that producers control their own activity. In this way, Proudhon, for example, said that the will of producers and workers to organize production by and for themselves constituted "the supreme revolutionary act." Anarchists make the same unyielding demand today; in conformity with all their principles and values, they demand that individuals enjoy the same freedom and the same equality in the economic field that they claim in all other spheres of human activity.

As we have seen, mutualism, federalism, and communism are diverse formulations that classical anarchists
developed in striving for the ideal of a just economy. More
generally, and beyond the various modalities of production
and distribution of goods that have been conceived, the
ideal of a truly democratic workplace, without hierarchy,
has been a constant of anarchist aspirations. According to
this ideal, people would work within a system of production
in which everyone has a say not only in what is produced
and consumed but also in the conditions of production and
consumption. Clearly, private ownership of the means of
production and the salary system—wage slavery—are perceived as disasters that must be immediately abolished.

These demands, deeply rooted in the very heart of
anarchism from the beginning of the movement, are in
acute contradiction to today's capitalism and the market
economy, just as they previously clashed with centrally
planned economies. In the latter case, anarchists very
quickly rejected the authoritarianism of these economies,
deploring their inefficiency, lack of democracy, and lack
of freedom. Following Bakunin, they predicted that these
economies would inevitably give rise to an oppressive
"coordinator" class. This prediction has been amply proven
accurate by history.

With the bankruptcy of the centrally planned economies,
the market economy was presented as the sole option for
the future. Most economists still cling to this idea that only
the market can coordinate economic activities in an efficient and humanly satisfying way. The most progressive
among them barely call for more than a bit of state intervention to palliate the worst failings and injustices engen-

dered by the market. Like Michael Albert, most anarchists reject this fatalism and continue to demand the abolition of the market and the establishment of a more just and more humane economy, in greater conformity with their values and ideals. Michael Albert has explained that "propaganda has convinced everyone of the benefits of the market. But I believe that the market is one of humanity's worst inventions. The structure and the dynamics of the market have necessarily spawned a long series of evils, from alienation to anti-social attitudes and behaviors and an unjust division of wealth. I am therefore an abolitionist of markets, though I know they will not disappear tomorrow, but in the same way I am an abolitionist of racism."

What should take its place and what do anarchists suggest? There are greatly divergent positions.

Some emphasize the inutility, uncertainty, and even harmfulness of constructing, in today's alienated and oppressed context, intricate models of how institutions will work in a liberated future. This is Noam Chomsky's perspective, and many arguments can be found to support it.

Others enter the debate in a more polemical and literary fashion, insisting on the imperative of freedom within anarchism and the necessity of embodying it here and now in the economic field. Bob Black's article on the abolition of work ("The Abolition of Work") is of this nature: "No one should ever work. Work is the source of nearly all the misery in the world. . . . That doesn't mean we have to stop doing things. It does mean creating a new way of life based on play . . ." This article in some ways resembles *Le Droit à la paresse* (*The Right to Be Lazy*, 1883) of Paul Lafargue: "Work, this strange madness which possesses the working classes. . . ." Black concluded, "No one should ever work. Workers of the world . . . *relax*!"

Still others evaluate historical experiences that have come close to meeting the ideal, encouraging these to be taken up or pursued. Among these are the kibbutzim, various experiments carried out during the Spanish Civil War, and currently the local exchange trading systems (LETS) that can be found in various parts of the world, in which people create their own money.

Even within the capitalist economy, the famous Mondragon Corporation in the Basque Country is an isolated but vibrant example of an efficient production site whose personnel are not organized according to the dominant management model.

Though marginal, more interesting examples can be found, promising future potential ruptures, diverse attempts to reestablish productive activities outside the profit model of the economy, such as the worker-managed factories in Argentina described in Naomi Klein and Avi Lewis's film *The Take*.

The anarchist ideal was forcefully reasserted by Robin Hahnel and Michael Albert in their stimulating work setting out a detailed model of a self-organized economy. Their goal was to show that this ideal is not only desirable but intellectually credible and practically viable. Drawing on the idea of workers' councils developed by Antonie Pannekoek and de Santillan particularly, Hahnel and Albert describe an economic model without profit, without a hierarchical organization of labor, and, of course, without the market. A detailed presentation of this model is outside the scope of this book, but it is nevertheless useful to provide an overview.

The authors start with the fundamental values of efficacy, solidarity, equity (of remuneration, but also of circumstances), participatory management, and diversity (results,
means, circumstances), and incorporate them into economic institutions ensuring production, allocation, and
consumption.

Concretely, this model relies on the creation of workers'
councils and consumers' councils at different levels, with
these elements: remuneration according to effort and sacrifice, the constitution of "balanced job complexes" (this is
fundamental: everyone takes on one of these complexes,
each of them being comparable to all the others), and participatory planning. Albert explained:

> We are proposing decentralized planning. People
> decide what they want to produce and consume
> and make their decisions knowing that each
> product uses raw materials and labour. The
> structure of work is also profoundly changed: no
> one has a single job, but a balanced job complex,
> all equally desirable. In other words, no one will
> want to consume something which requires
> disgusting jobs because that will make their own
> job less interesting. Finally, in such a model, prices
> reflect the social cost of production; this does not
> presuppose a perfect concurrence nor that people
> are saints.

This model, whose viability has been tested on the theoretical level, has in fact been implemented; notably by a
publishing company (South End Press) and a Canadian

cooperative (Arbeiter Ring). These experiments definitely merit close observation. However, although Chomsky is a close associate of these ideas and even a longtime neighbor, he has consistently refused to take a position on Hahnel and Albert's participatory economics:

> Do we know enough to respond in great detail to questions about the eventual functioning of a society? It seems to me that responses to this type of question must be discovered through experience. Take, for example, the market economy. . . . I understand the critiques very well; but they are not sufficient to show that a system which eliminates the market would be preferable, that's an elementary point of logic. We simply don't have any answers to this type of question.

Anarcho-Syndicalism

After 1890, anarchists made huge inroads into the unions, especially in the Latin American countries, developing an anarchist form of syndicalism called anarcho-syndicalism. This movement became very large and powerful, and for a time played a leading role in workers' movements and social struggles. It had repercussions and impacts on the entire union movement in many countries. Except for the case of Spain, where the CNT remained active until the civil war, anarcho-syndicalism constituted a major force until its decline with the First World War.

I will focus on the French experience, which is representative of the anarcho-syndicalist venture—the grounds on which it was initiated, and its strengths, weaknesses, and impact.

The workers' movement began to reorganize itself in Europe in the nineteenth century. Labor organization was rethought, and its practices repositioned in light of the new political, social, and economic conditions established through the Industrial Revolution. Numerous conceptualizations of syndicalism were advanced, often concurrently: reformist or revolutionary, linked to a political party or apolitical, internationalist or not, and so on. For example, the communists unsurprisingly wanted a syndicalism that was, according to Lenin, "a conveyor belt of party directives."

Anarchists remained outside these debates for some time. In their view, the ad hoc and reformist nature of union struggles made them immediately incompatible with anarchist goals. Isn't demanding a wage increase an implicit recognition of the right to hire and thus a perpetuation of wage slavery, as it was then commonly called? Isn't demanding reform an implicit acknowledgment that the authorities have the right to grant it? If union action was only about seeking better working conditions and salaries, anarchists refused to enter into this logic. Moreover, syndicalism linked to a political party, even a socialist party, in their view inevitably degenerated into parliamentarianism and bourgeois and reformist policies.

However, a decision to get involved in the unions was made at the beginning of the 1890s. One of the most brilliant defenders of this position was Fernand Pelloutier (1867–1901), who died of exhaustion at age thirty-two. He remains, along with Émile Pouget and Rudolf Rocker, one of the most important activists and theorists of anarcho-syndicalism.

Pelloutier was convinced that anarchists should be active in the unions. Two things encouraged this course of action. The first was the failure of "propaganda by the deed," which most workers and anarchist activists condemned. The second was that the split of the socialist ranks into diverse currents lent increasing credibility to an apolitical concept of syndicalism, opposed to any collaboration with the state. This was precisely the position promoted by the anarchists. Pelloutier was at first involved in the *Bourses du travail* (labor exchanges), created in 1893. These were meant to be a kind of workers' equivalent to chambers of commerce, uniting all workers within a given territory. The labor exchanges were to become a space to learn direct action and self-liberation; they aimed to "monopolize all services for bettering the lot of the working class." In addition to all the services directly related to work, there was a magazine, *L'Ouvrier des deux mondes* (*The Worker from Two Worlds*), and open universities. Pelloutier was in fact a great believer in education, stating that syndicalism should "educate to revolt" and provide the worker with "the science of his unhappiness."

In 1895, the *Confédération générale du travail* (CGT; General Confederation of Labor) was founded at a congress in Limoges. Eighteen labor exchanges participated. Gradually a revolutionary concept of syndicalism gained ground, based on a double structure of unions uniting workers from the same sector at the national level, and the labor exchanges uniting workers from the same city. The CGT's Ninth Congress adopted the famous Charter of Amiens (1906), which set out the principles, goals, and means of this direct-action syndicalism, rejecting the necessity and expediency of having intermediaries between bosses and workers. These free associations of free producers aimed to bring about the social revolution outside party politics. While they sought an improvement in the conditions of their members, this was only an aspect of their work. The ultimate goal of the unions was "the disappearance of the salary system and of bosses." They believed that "the complete emancipation of workers can only be achieved by expropriating the capitalists." After this expropriation, these groupings of struggle and resistance were destined to become "groupings of production and redistribution, the basis for social reorganization." At that point, union members would naturally be "anti-vote" and "antiwar."

The recommended means were sabotage (badly done work, breaking machines, etc); the oft-adopted practices of boycott and labeling (a symbol granted to an employer by a union in return for his commitment to social conventions); and striking, leading up to a general strike, the instrument of revolution. Pelloutier was able to cite Bakunin, Proudhon, and Kropotkin in support of anarcho-syndicalism. However, other anarchists remained hostile or at least reserved. During a famous debate between Malatesta and the young Pierre Monatte in Amsterdam in 1907, Malatesta proclaimed, "We must be wary of any unilateral action. Syndicalism, however excellent it may be for motivating the working class, can never be the sole method of anarchism."

The conceptions and practices of revolutionary syndicalism greatly fueled the union movement in its beginnings, later losing out to reformist strategies. However, with the increasingly noticeable integration and institutionalization of the big labor confederations, wage earners are rediscovering the ideas and practice of direct-action syndicalism from the beginning of the century. This is owing to new tools of struggle, such as the coordinations of the 1980s (rail workers, nurses) and alternative unions (the SUD and CGT in France, the Cobas in Italy, the CNT in Spain, etc.).

Ecology

Ecology is a scientific discipline of biology that studies, according to the usual definition (given by Ernst Haeckel in 1866), "the relations between living beings and the world around them." The results and conclusions of this science have concerned us more closely since disturbing observations about the health of our planet have become a matter of daily concern: pollution, global warming, ecosystem destruction, deforestation, etc. Ecology thus comes back to values and a social and political project. Lest anyone be tempted to forget, it must be stressed that severe and justified criticisms have constantly been leveled at some conceptions of so-called deep ecology and the practices they have inspired. They have rightly been denounced for their antihumanism and irrationality.

Ecological concerns are fairly recent and, it must be admitted, received hardly any attention from the first anarchists. However, as we know, some of these were geographers. It is thus not surprising that we can discover in their writings certain emphases and a sensitivity prefiguring some of the ecological concerns that have now become widespread.

For example, Élisée Reclus wrote in his compendium

The Earth and Its Inhabitants,

> Our liberty, in our relations with the earth, consists of recognizing its laws in order to bring our existence into conformity with them. Whatever the relative ease of manner that has conquered our intelligence and will, we remain no less the products of the planet, tied to its surface like imperceptible animalcules, carried along by all its movements and dependent on its laws.

However, an anarchist concept of ecology that was both rationalist and humanist remained to be developed. The development of this ecology, avoiding the excesses of deep ecology and the timidity of reformist ecologies, was the work of Murray Bookchin (1921–2006).

Bookchin believed the root of the problem lay in the psychology of domination, which arose with patriarchy, slavery, and the first primitive cities of the Neolithic period. His analysis began with this historical observation:

> The domination of the human by the human preceded the idea of dominating nature. . . . The hierarchies, classes, forms of property, and statist institutions which emerged with social domination have been transposed onto humanity's relation with nature. Nature tends to be considered as no more than a resource, raw material to be freely exploited.

Bookchin, in this way, rejected both the timid reformism

of those he called "environmentalists"—those who conveniently mask the social and institutional causes of our ecological problems—as well as the antihumanism within the tenets of deep ecology, which he believed led to irrationality: The two points of view make humanity appear to be the enemy of nature, whether as calamity or lord. For his part, Bookchin developed an approach known as libertarian municipalism. It has the great merit of not imposing the terrible choice between "lobbies, compromise, and bargaining" on the one hand and "a biocentric mentality" on the other.

In response to those who might be attracted by the former, he forcefully argued that talk about "limits to growth" in the context of a capitalist market economy was as meaningless as talk about weapons controls in a warrior society. The fine sentiments expressed by well-intentioned environmentalists are as naïve as those expressed by multinationals are manipulative. Convincing capitalism to limit its growth is as likely as convincing someone to stop breathing. All attempts to establish "green capitalism" or "ecological capitalism" in the name of elusive "sustainable development" are bound to fail because of the very nature of the capitalist system, by definition a system of infinite growth.

To those swayed by deep ecology, Bookchin summoned the rationalist heritage of the Enlightenment against all forms of a "philosophy" that celebrated irrationality, instinct, and religiosity by cultivating a hatred of humanity and a love for nature, including pathogenic viruses whose "unalienable rights" have been defended by deep ecologists, as Bookchin noted.

Bookchin's libertarian municipalism aimed to define

what he called an "ecological society." He conceived it as structured around an ecological society, structured around a confederated commune of communes, each of which is shaped to conform with the ecosystem and bioregion in which it is located, would deploy this ensemble of technologies in an artistic way. It would make use of local resources, many of which have been abandoned because of mass production techniques.

One of the undeniable merits of Bookchin's work is that he offered concrete and credible solutions, tackling and analyzing the problems he examined in depth. It followed that his ecological project was inseparable from a political project. His project rejected the idea that the "only response to technology run wild" was a "return to hunting and gathering"; it also denounced the "logic of modern science and engineering" informing our current political and social institutions as a celebration of irrationalism.

Education

In the wake of the French Revolution, starting in the nineteenth century, national and state systems of education began to be established in every part of the world. This was perceived as a project and a victory of the left. It is still true today that attacks on such systems essentially come from the right.

However, from the very beginning, though they did still recognize its potential benefits, anarchists raised strong critiques of this project—though of course not because of any sympathy with elitism or in defense of the old aristocratic order.

It was inevitable that antiauthoritarians would from the outset recognize the dangers and threats to liberty inherent in the very idea of national education—and they were more or less the only leftists to do so with unceasing insistence. They soon saw it as state appropriation of children's minds. What could be expected from such an education other than training in passive behavior? What could be expected other than the sacrifice of freedom on the altar of conformism, of creativity on that of group-think, of solidarity on that of narrow nationalism and ethnocentrism? Couldn't it be foreseen that it would lead to the manufacture of docile individuals, obedient to masters and especially bosses, who would complacently—and the First World War provided decisive and bloody proof of this—go and die on the front as soon as the order was given? William Godwin and Max Stirner first expressed these misgivings. From different perspectives, each wrote extensively on the question of national education. They forcefully argued that such a project would entail indoctrination in the social, political, and economic order and that it could constitute a deathblow to critical thinking and individual autonomy.

All anarchists necessarily followed suit, sharing their distrust, if not always their analysis. Most anarchists still subscribe to Bertrand Russell's view that "men are born ignorant, not stupid. They are made stupid by education." Similarly, Noam Chomsky said, "Education is a system of imposed ignorance."

Anarchists make no mistake about the decisive importance of education, however: like previous revolutionary movements, anarchists believe that education is essential to achieve the social change desired. Better still—and this is what distinguishes it from other revolutionary movements—anarchists are not content with a theory of education but have, since very early on, sought to establish concrete models of education based on anarchist theory. Since Godwin, the history of the anarchist movement has thus included concrete pedagogical projects, from establishing schools and teaching institutions to the development of pedagogical material and the publication of journals and periodicals for children.

Sébastien Faure's La Ruche, Paul Robin's Cempuis, Leo Tolstoy's Yasnaya Polyana, Bertrand Russell's Beacon Hill, and Alexander Neill's Summerhill are among the best known of these schools.

These projects emerged from ongoing thought and discussion about pedagogy. The main ideas, which crystallized between 1880 and 1914, are summarized here.

As other works by Michael P. Smith have shown, anarchists believe that education must possess five essential and complementary characteristics: education must be holistic, multidisciplinary, rational, emancipatory, and permanent.

That education must be holistic—an idea that can be traced to Charles Fourier (1772–1837)—means that it must address all aspects of a human being. The division between manual and intellectual education was (and for the most part, still is) very socially marked. Anarchists fundamentally reject this cleavage. Their schools have thus tried to alternate, in a complementary and congruent way, manual and intellectual teaching: workshop and classroom, lessons in words and lessons in things.

Education must at the same time be multidisciplinary. The future worker must be effectively prepared to navigate the dangers of the labor market, particularly those arising from the division of labor. For anarchists, there is no question of training for only one occupation. They advocate a multidisciplinary education as a matter of liberty and autonomy.

Education must be rational. The scientific and rationalist aspect of anarchism comes to the fore here. The kind of education promoted by anarchists is of course secular and humanist, independent of both church and state. Moreover, it places science at the heart of the pedagogical project. In an era before the advent of destructive technoscience and ideological scientism, anarchists called for education in which science was a force for liberation from superstitions and a major and formative intellectual exercise, a guarantor of both material and human progress. Their defense and practice of sexual education—freeing minds from prejudice, accepting birth control, ensuring harmonious and free sexual life—is exemplary of what they hoped for from teaching based on science and reason.

Such an education would be emancipatory. It would form the conditions for the free exercise of reason in every individual and pave the way for a social life in which the exercise of one person's freedom relies on respect for the freedoms of everyone else.

In its own way, by its own means, education must also contribute to preparing for a world freed from its current restrictions and servitudes.

Within this stream of thought, anarchists have experimented with diverse academic and pedagogical formulas. It has sometimes been argued that the academy is destined to disappear in favor of collective and permanent education. The anarcho-syndicalists' labor exchanges gave form and life to this idea.

Anarchists initiated and promoted numerous innovations (mixed classes, rejection of physical force, student
participation in the democratic life of the institution, etc.),
most of which are now standard practice. Moreover, it is
no coincidence that anarchists first lucidly examined the
difficult and recurrent question of authority in education.
As all educators are aware, the issue of legitimate authority
arises with special urgency in the field of education. What
can be imposed? By what right? How and to what ends?
The task of educating young and vulnerable minds raises
these questions; anarchism has no simple or general
answers. Nevertheless, antiauthoritarianism and love of
freedom require a particular sensitivity to this question and
an attempt to analytically address it. Once again, Bakunin
is very clear on this:

> The entire education of children and their instruction
> must be based on the scientific development of
> reason, not on faith; on the development of dignity
> and personal interdependence, and not of piety and
> obedience; on respect for truth and justice and,
> above all, on human respect which must replace,
> in everything and everywhere, worship of the
> divine. The principle of authority in the education
> of children provides a natural starting point.
> Applied to very young children, whose intelligence
> is not yet fully developed, it is legitimate. But
> development, including that of education, implies
> the successive negation of this starting point; the
> principle must yield to rising freedom as education
> and instruction advance. All rational education is

in essence the progressive eradication of authority in favor of liberty, since the overall objective of education should be the formation of free men, full of respect and love for the liberty of others.

Any study of anarchist ideas about, and practices of, education must include Francisco Ferrer I Guardia (1859–1909), a martyr of anarchist history. Ferrer, of Catalan origin, was exiled to Paris at a young age due to his anarchist ideas and activism. He then made his living by giving Spanish lessons.

This exile ended in 1901 and Ferrer returned to Spain. A bequest from a Parisian student allowed him to pursue his dream of opening a modern school in Barcelona, partly inspired by similar anarchist experiments unfolding in France at that time. He was also able to open a publishing house dedicated to anarchist ideas in education. In 1907, Ferrer was imprisoned after an attack on Alphonse XIII. He was quickly released for lack of evidence. However, in the summer of 1909, as violent riots broke out in Barcelona to protest sending troops to Morocco, Ferrer was again arrested, on August 31. This time, a trial was pushed through and a huge international protest movement was unable to stop Ferrer's execution on October 31, 1909. Ferrer's trial was reopened two years later and in 1912 his conviction declared a "mistake."

Ferrer's ideas in rational education, and his educational practices in the modern school movement greatly contributed to the history of contemporary education, prefiguring many of the issues and practices ushered in by the pedagogical experiments of the interwar period and the 1960s. He wrote:

We want people who are capable of continually evolving,
capable of renewing both their environment and
themselves; people whose intellectual independence
will be their greatest strength and who will always
be inclined to agree with what is preferable, happy at
the triumph of new and right ideas. . . . Society fears
such beings; we cannot hope that it will consent to an
education capable of training them.

These ideas, with roots in the ideals of rationalism and
emancipation of the Enlightenment, were to a great extent
integrated into the educational theories and practices of the
twentieth century. However, the radicalism that inspired
them, and their roots in an antistate project of social transformation, were forgotten. They nevertheless remain central to anarchist thinking on education, and until recently
were very broadly held to be self-evident. For anarchists, it
was essential to situate education within a broader project
of forming free, equal, and sovereign individuals. In this
way, they strongly insisted on the irreducibility of education to any kind of functional adaptation of individuals to
the surrounding world—or, worse, to the labor market.

Chomsky has recalled that John Dewey (a Democrat who
was in no sense a revolutionary, but undoubtedly the most
important philosopher of education in the United States
during the past century) took it for granted that "vocational
and professional perspectives" would deliver "university
and education, bound hand and foot" to what he called the
"captains of industry." Dewey strongly rejected such a concept of education, which he saw as serving no other purpose than forming "docile pawns," with only a "narrow,"

"practical" education directly linked to employment, and ensuring that individuals were predisposed to believe that "company efficacy makes any consideration of workplace democracy inappropriate and out of the question." It was in opposition to this "vocational" concept of education, against education dominated by "business for the growth of profits, reinforced by the media, its agents and all other means of publicity and propaganda" that Dewey developed his democratic ideal of education. This was based on another axiom, today considered utopic in certain circles: "The chief vocation of all human beings . . . is moral and intellectual growth"; in other words, the ultimate goal of education being the attempt to produce, "not goods, but free human beings associating with each other on the basis of equality."

With the current subjugation of education to business and in the context of a general commercialization of education, we are on the brink of forgetting the fundamental fact that the primary role of education is not a matter of integrating individuals into the workforce and the economic order. If today's ideological blinkers make the otherwise banal ideas of Dewey appear radical, it says a great deal about the world in which we live. To use a single example, the submission of the public university to the interests of private tyrannies is all but taken for granted; it neither requires justification nor arouses indignation.

Contemporary anarchist thought continues to expand our horizons. After the idea was launched, by Ivan Illich and John Holt in particular (best known in the Anglo-Saxon world), anarchists have been intently observing, or in some cases participating in, "unschooling" projects in most Western countries. This perspective is now shared by hundreds of thousands, many of whom are far from anarchist. They believe that it is better for children to leave school and begin to learn freely by themselves, and with others, using the innumerable means currently available to learn and acquire a real education.

Direct action and self-organization once again help inform this practice, which rejects state indoctrination and its coterie of experts and officials in favor of freedom and the joy of learning.

Anarchist analysis and contributions in the area of education have gone far beyond educational institutions for children. Higher education and university have also been, and remain, of concern. Anarchists are inclined to describe the university as an institution dedicated to preventing certain questions from arising and ensuring the domination of the masters and the reproduction of a class of intellectuals and coordinators ready to follow orders.

More generally still, anarchists have raised questions about the place of intellectual and cultural life in our societies. Most anarchists would agree that Bakunin was justified in predicting a dictatorship of academics and experts.

"Worst of all," he said, "to be slaves of pedants, what a future for humanity! Give these academics a free hand to dispose of the lives of others and they will subject society to the same experiments they now use on rabbits, cats, and dogs in the name of science."

From the same perspective, Chomsky has written that for over 200 years, "experiments" have been conducted by the powerful following the highest principles of economic science, with startlingly uniform results: benefits for the experimenters and their power base, tragedies for the experimental animals.

In our times, education is not the only means used to achieve these same ends, including the attempt to exclude the public from debates that concern them and to empty the concept of democracy of all content. While other means play a role, the media are central.

Media

To start, let's note several important but little-known facts that Noam Chomsky has often cited.

The entry of the United States into the First World War required a shift in public opinion, which was fiercely opposed to war. To achieve this, the American government established the Committee on Public Information, also known as the Creel Commission, which successfully undertook the task of shaping minds as necessary to change public opinion. The members of the commission had the entire range of propaganda techniques then available at their disposal and even devised a few of their own. The birth of the public relations industry, currently flourishing and possessing extraordinary power, can be traced to this project and those who implemented it. It was in this context that a certain conception of the media—of their role and function in manufacturing consent within advanced industrial societies—developed. These early pioneers made no attempt to conceal their propagandist aims. In his aptly entitled article, "Propaganda," Chomsky recalled that in one of the first editions of the *Encyclopedia of Social Sciences* in the 1930s, one of its most prestigious researchers, Harold Lasswell, discussed the relationship between the media and democracy. Lasswell warned against succumbing to what he called "democratic dogmatism"—that is, the notion that ordinary people are capable of determining their own needs and interests, thus of choosing what is best for themselves. According to Lasswell, this idea was completely false and the truth was that others—an elite to which the author doubtless felt certain he belonged—must decide for them. Tiresomely, however, we live in a democracy and it is not possible to control the population by force. Happily, Lasswell and his peers had a solution at hand: instead of force, the population could be perfectly controlled by propaganda and persuasion.

In light of this, Edward S. Herman and Noam Chomsky presented and tested a "model of propaganda" in their book *Manufacturing Consent.*

According to this model, the media are essentially overdetermined by various structural and institutional factors that the authors call filters. These shape—not entirely but extensively—the type of representation of reality that the mainstream media offer, as well as the values, norms, and perceptions they promote. According to this analysis, the media, "serves to mobilize support for particular interests which dominate the actions of the state and the private sector; their choices, emphasis and omissions can be better understood—and sometimes understood in an exemplary manner with striking clarity—when they are analysed in these terms."

A systematic and highly political dichotomization can be observed in the media coverage of events, reflecting the interests of the most powerful. Let's briefly summarize the five filters of the propaganda model of the media.

The first filter consists of the size, ownership, and profit orientation of the media.

The second is the dependence of the media on publicity: the media does not so much sell information to the public as sell the public to advertisers. In this way, those who buy a daily newspaper have themselves become, generally without suspecting it, a significant part of the product, while they believe they are simply buying information.

The third filter is created by the dependence of the media on certain sources of information: government, businesses themselves (notably through increasingly important public relations firms), lobby groups, and media agencies. Together this creates, through symbiosis (if we can call it that), a sort of bureaucratic and ideological affinity between the media and those who feed them.

The fourth filter is "flack"; that is, criticism by the powerful that serves to discipline the media. Briefly, there is a tendency to recognize certain, commonly accepted sources as trustworthy. Both work and potential criticism are spared by relying almost exclusively on these sources and lending credibility to their image of expertise. What these sources and experts say is factual; what others say is opinion, commentary, subjective, and, by definition, of lesser value. Naturally, all of this commentary is broadly circumscribed by the preceding context.

Herman and Chomsky called the fifth and last filter anticommunism—a label obviously influenced by the American context of the time. It refers more generally to the hostility of media to all leftist, socialist, and progressive perspectives.

This model of the media does not suggest any kind

of conspiracy but presents an intellectual construct that requires no motivations—secret or otherwise—to explain what takes place. And what takes place, if this model is correct, is a remarkable form of mind control, allowing full liberty within fixed frameworks: a kind of consensual self-censorship, the most effective of all forms of censorship. In sum, the media contributes enormously to establishing and defending the status quo. It serves the masters' interests through the choice of issues, the importance it assigns them, and the way in which the issues are treated—filtering information, highlighting certain aspects, and tone. All within certain acceptable premises.

This model has been severely criticized. It has been attacked for its limited nature, provoking the objection that it does not account for the great diversity of media practices in reality. Journalists have vehemently countered with their own experience, rightly asserting there is no trace of censorship in their field. Academics in media and other fields have warned that such a model comes dangerously close to positing a more or less secret conspiracy, which we would have to admit is hardly credible.

For the most part, however, these critiques seem to arise from a profound misunderstanding of the authors' intent. It is true that their model, as a whole, is far from reflecting the diverse practices of the media world. However, it does not claim to do so. Similarly, it does not pretend to address the actors in an overarching or significant way. The feeling of complete freedom that the journalists experience is no doubt quite real; but this experience in no way contradicts the theory, which is on a different level of analysis. Finally, the authors have been clear that there is no question of a conspiracy here: everything is out in the open and can be explained entirely by the institutions involved and their dynamics.

In the end, the crucial question is whether observation conforms to prediction. It seems that it does, and impeccably so. The authors carry out a detailed analysis of media production on a variety of issues, and the results prove remarkably true to their predictions.

Once more we can quote Chomsky:

> What would be the null hypothesis, the kind of conjecture that you'd make assuming nothing further. The obvious assumption is that the product of the media, what appears, what doesn't appear, the way it is slanted, will reflect the interest of the buyers and sellers, the institutions, and the power systems that are around them. If that wouldn't happen, it would be kind of a miracle. Okay, then comes the hard work. You ask, does it work the way you predict? Well, you can judge for yourselves. There's lots of material on this obvious hypothesis, which has been subjected to the hardest tests anybody can think of, and still stands up remarkably well. You virtually never find anything in the social sciences that so strongly supports any conclusion, which is not a big surprise, because it would be miraculous if it didn't hold up given the way the forces are operating.

This leads to a practical question of great importance. If we take the propaganda model of the media seriously, and if we share the vision of democracy as a political regime in which well-informed citizens are invited to play an active, significant, critical, and thoughtful part in matters that affect the common good, what should we do? After a quick glance at the global media situation, at the increasing concentration of ownership, and at the kind of ideology being promoted, it becomes clear that this question is not in the least rhetorical but one that requires urgent attention.

There are many possible responses to this crucial question, but examining these lies outside the scope of this book. For now, we can simply say that an education providing a solid base of general culture, developing critical thinking, or perhaps adding education about the media to the curriculum has a reasonable chance of acting as an antidote to media propaganda. Use of alternative media should be promoted to train and develop critical thought.

Finally, it is perhaps most important to break the isolation, exchange with others, and learn from each other. Activism is an invaluable school and definitely the most effective of all antidotes against the isolation and lack of critical thought instilled by these tools of the elite.

Ethics

Anarchists have proposed and defended a panoply of values and explored innumerable avenues of morality. It would be fruitless to attempt to discern any kind of doctrinal unity in this area.

Throughout the history of anarchism, values have been lived and promulgated—and it is in this sense that we can speak of anarchist morals. Anarchists have also attempted to systematize these values and legitimize their choices;

in this sense, there are anarchist ethics. Finally, anarchists have also turned to ethics itself: attempting to clarify the nature of ethics, identify its origins, and elucidate the basis for ethical judgments. In this sense, we can refer to an anarchist metaethics.

Examining all of these practices and theories, two characteristics stand out. The first, pretty much a constant, is the value placed on individual autonomy and, in particular, free and independent judgment capable of resisting the pressure to bow to a servility that would render all morality impossible. This is hardly surprising, given that the critical questioning of authority is at the heart of anarchist morality and ethics. All familiar with Stanley Milgram's (1933–1984) famous experiment in social psychology—*Obedience to Authority* (1974)—can't fail to recognize the relevance of this starting point.

A second prominent characteristic is the austerity marking most anarchist moral positions. In the past as well as today, we generally find a rejection of alcohol and tobacco, pacifism and nonviolence, vegetarianism, green consumerism, primitivism (that is, a voluntary return to the simple life), and so on. This extends to lifestyle activism, as it is called in Anglo-Saxon countries, which takes multiple forms and attempts to ascribe moral and then political significance to the most mundane activities. It is in this sense that anarchism can be said—in my view, without being entirely mistaken—to constitute a political return to Immanuel Kant and his puritanical rigor.

As Maletesta wrote, "Anarchism is born of a moral revolt against social injustice." This attitude implies the promotion and defense of values dear to anarchists: notably, freedom, equality, equity, solidarity, and tolerance. Anarchist ethics are an attempt to systematize this and on this level, the positions of individualist and social anarchists can easily be distinguished.

Within the tradition of anarchist individualism, there is an ethic of self-realization and authenticity, which draws on Stirner and his egoism to struggle against mutilations of the I by law, society, state, religion, prejudice, and superstition. The positions of individualists have very often been subject to caricature. Until recently, it is true that the positions they took were controversial, especially on sexual morality though much of these are now banal. However, it should not be forgotten that their concept of self-pleasure was wedded to rigor and authenticity and the will to escape from the slavery of vice as well as virtue. The morality of individualist anarchists has never meant anything goes. The worker that Arvon described could be a typical anarchist individualist: "Participating assiduously in study groups and a fervent self-learner, he desires to owe his emancipation to none but his own efforts. While he may hold society and the state responsible for his humiliation, he never forgets that the primary condition for his rehabilitation is his own labour of self-perfection."

Morality and ethics based on the I, however, is limited. In my view, social anarchism offers more significant anarchist contributions. Their most striking feature is the attempt to naturalize ethics, even seeking to develop a science of morality in some cases. Here liberty consists in conformity to this "natural law" not being impeded. This naturalization takes various forms. Tolstoy seeks it within a unique interpretation of Christian brotherhood. For Proudhon, it lies in the idea of justice: "Feel, affirm human dignity; first, in all that pertains to us, then in your neighbor, without egoistic gain and without any thought of divinity or community: this is the law. Be ready, in all circumstances, to take and to defend this dignity, even when necessary against oneself: this is justice." I'll limit myself to citing a few aspects of Kropotkin's exemplary thought.

In the first place, Kropotkin was inspired by Adam Smith, who is now known almost exclusively as the author of *The Wealth of Nations*. Dominant ideology propagates a distorted reading of this book and makes Smith the high priest of unhindered market expansion and its invisible hand. This is false, and anyone who makes the effort to read will realize that Smith was primarily a moralist whose work on the economy is meaningless without reference to his ethics. For Smith, the "sentiment of sympathy" is the origin of moral sentiment. For Kropotkin, this constituted a major intellectual breakthrough. "You see a man beat a child. You know that the beaten child suffers. Your imagination makes you feel the pain inflicted on him yourself, or his tears and his little suffering face tell you of it. If you are not a coward, you snatch him away from the brute. This example in itself explains almost all moral sentiments."

Kropotkin believed that Smith, lacking a knowledge of biology, had not been able to fully ground his position in nature. At the end of the last century, however, several authors elaborated an ideology of social Darwinism, in which competition and the struggle of one against all were taken as the basis of human behavior. From this starting point, they attempted to justify a social and political order modeled on the jungle, in which only the "strongest" and "fittest" would survive. Kropotkin objected strenuously, writing *Mutual Aid: A Factor of Evolution*. He argued that the natural law of species is primarily a law of mutual aid and cooperation, suggesting that the moral and political positions of anarchists are in harmony with this natural order.

The book is excellent and of greater interest in an era when the long despised concept of human nature is being everywhere rediscovered. However, do we agree with Kropotkin that, because the natural order is preponderantly informed by the practice of mutual aid, our institutions should follow suit? Does it necessarily follow that the social and political order should conform to what is said to be the natural order?

In fact, to deduce from the biological fact of mutual aid and cooperation the necessity of a society without a state (which would then allow this character to flourish) is a paralogism. This fallacy has been known since it was exposed by David Hume; it is one to which all naturalistic approaches to ethics are prone. Hume taught that descriptive judgments do not translate into prescriptive judgments; we cannot deduce "what must be" from "what is."

It is important to recognize that ethical questions are among the most difficult, and very little is known about them. Kropotkin, no more than other anarchists, does not provide convincing responses. In my view, this in no way diminishes the nobility of the ideal the anarchists have handed down to us; nor does it reduce the real interest and currency of the questions they raise, particularly those initiated by Kropotkin and continued in some ways by Noam Chomsky.

In an interview, Tor Wennerberg asked Chomsky to clarify his thinking on the question of the genetic determination of language capabilities and its implications for morality. Chomsky replied,

> Well, for one thing, I don't think it can really be much of a question. (That's not to say we understand anything about it.) But, the fact of the matter is that we're constantly making moral judgments in new situations, and over a substantial range we do it in a convergent fashion—we don't differ randomly and wildly from one another. Furthermore, young children do it, very quickly, and they also converge. Of course, there are cultural and social and historical effects, but even for those to operate, they must be operating on something. If you look at this range of phenomena, there are only two possibilities: one is, it's a miracle, and the other is, it's rooted in our nature. It's rooted in our nature in the same sense in which language is, or for that matter, having arms and legs is. And it takes different forms depending on the circumstances, just as arms and legs depend on nutrition, and language depends on my not having heard Swedish when I was six months old and so on.

Anarcho-Feminism

Anarchism and feminism have been indelibly linked since 1792, when Mary Wollstonecraft published *A Vindication of the Rights of Women*. Generations of anarchists who followed, from Louise Michel, Voltairine de Cleyre, Emma Goldman, and Lucy Parsons, have taken up, deepened, and renewed an anarchist analysis of the situation of women.

Anarchism by definition is opposed to all illegitimate forms of authority and would be self-contradictory indeed if it failed to reject sexism (as well as racism, homophobia, and all other forms of discrimination). Any consistent anarchist is necessarily feminist. It is far from the case, however, that all anarchists have grasped this point of logical coherence, nor have they integrated all its theoretical and practical implications. The machismo of Proudhon is well known, but it should also be noted that most "classical" anarchists held conservative views on the conditions of women.

While it is true that all anarchists are properly feminist, not all feminists are anarchist.

It is entirely possible to adopt a feminist position demanding equal access to power for women or a position that power be held exclusively by women. It is on this point that anarcho-feminism diverges from other types of feminism. Anarcho-feminists do not only seek true liberation, nor greater or more equal participation of women in power, nor even the establishment of a "matriarchy." They seek no less than the elimination of illegitimate power in general and of the state in particular. For this reason, anarcho-feminism is very critical of reformist struggles that demand no more than "equal opportunity" for women in a context that remains "archaic." On the question of the vote for women, Emma Goldman thus took the following position:

> She can give suffrage or the ballot no new quality, nor can she receive anything from it that will enhance her own quality. Her development, her freedom, her independence must come from and through herself. First by asserting herself as a

personality, and not as a sex commodity. Second, by refusing to anyone the right over her body; by refusing to bear children, unless she wants them; by refusing to be a servant to God, the State, society, the husband, the family, etc.

The movement of "free women" (*Mujeres libres*) in the Spanish Civil War is a notable episode in the history of anarcho-feminism. Martha Ackelsberg has closely studied the fight of these women against sexism in the CNT and FAI and its masculine members, and in support of a greater and more significant participation of women in the Spanish anarchist movement. In the same vein as Goldman, Federica Montseny wrote that feminism was wrong to limit itself to "wanting to grant women of a specific class the opportunity to participate more actively in a system of privileges of rank" and that if these institutions "are injust when they are used to profit men, they remain unjust when women profit from them."

Peggy Kornegger and others have noted that, from the 1960s on, feminism has shared many commonalities with anarchism; in analysis and demands as well as preferred modes of action. At a more fundamental level, anarcho-feminists have helped expose the eminently political—that is, institutionally overdetermined—nature of many aspects of what was hitherto considered the strictly personal life of women. Thus they actively participated in nonhierarchical groups that were established and which practiced direct action. There they reaffirmed their belief that it is within authoritarian social structures and institutions that the oppression of women must be sought out and combated.

In sum, these activists and thinkers enriched anarchism, integrating new thought and practice on a broad variety of issues, such as marriage, the nuclear family, birth and education of children, parental roles and more. This opened an entire dimension of social life, previously lamentably neglected by anarchism, to analysis and action. As Ko negger wrote, anarcho-feminism basically

> postulates the nuclear family as the basis for all authoritarian systems. The lesson the child learns, from father to teacher to boss to God, is to OBEY the great anonymous voice of Authority. To graduate from childhood to adulthood is to become a full-fledged automaton, incapable of questioning or even thinking clearly.

Finally, and this is not their least achievement, anarcho-feminists have exposed how easily practice can contradict theory and even sincere anarchists can succumb to authoritarianism and sexism.

Anarcho-capitalism (sic)

Under this strange label, uniting two irreducibly opposed concepts, there has emerged in the past decades an ideological trend that has had particular traction in the United States. It aims to extend "the freedom of anarchism to the economy" and to "deploy capitalist freedom throughout the social order," according to Pierre Lemieux, one of its best French-language representatives. In brief, this view holds that, again in Lemieux's words, a "capitalist society without a state is economically efficient and morally desirable."

I should clarify from the outset that this ideology hardly merits more than a footnote in this book explaining why it should be given no more consideration than oxymorons such as a free slave or the living dead. However, two crucial facts prevent me from leaving it at that.

The first is that anarcho-capitalist positions belong to a growing family of ideas exercising increasing allure. This ideological family includes libertarians, adherents of the *Austrian School* of *economics* and—almost exclusively in the United States—followers of Ayn Rand, the novelist and essayist of Russian origin. Although it must be acknowledged that there are some important nuances among these different currents, they all call for the retreat of the state, particularly from the economy. It could thus be argued that this ideological family in fact belongs to the dominant ideology, and that certain of its ideas play a not at all negligible role in defining public policy.

The second reason militating against a too-rapid dismissal of anarcho-capitalist concepts is that its authors and thinkers present themselves as anarchists. Such intellectual dishonesty cannot be allowed to pass unchallenged.

Let's start by reviewing anarcho-capitalist positions. Anarcho-capitalism traces its roots to economic liberalism and political liberalism. In the area of economics, their primary inspiration is the interpretation of the market developed by Austrian school economists. According to Ludwig von Mises and Friedrich Hayek, the market, pure and unobstructed by state intervention, is a "catallaxy," an abstract mode of managing information, which produces an optimal, spontaneous order that no organization or planning could hope to achieve. In the abstract, it presupposes freedom for all, rights for all, and, thus, according to its zealots, delivers both justice and freedom.

These latter ideas are owed to political liberalism and particularly its concept of jus naturalism. This is a concept of rights first developed by John Locke. In essence, anarcho-capitalists argue that individuals have a natural right (hence jus naturalism) over their person, the products of their labor as well as natural resources they discover or transform. From this perspective, other rights become superfluous or even harmful. The right to life, for example, is essentially the right not to be killed; it in no way implies access to resources necessary to well-being.

In response to all these other rights, anarcho-capitalists (and libertarians) tend to oppose what they describe as paternalism of state institutions, which undermines individual responsibility. In their view, these latter are coercive and, in any case, ineffective.

The anarcho-capitalist doctrine—whose principal representatives are currently Murray Rothbard, Robert Nozick, and David Friedman—rests on these two pillars.

Anarcho-capitalists imagine a society without a state, and the vitriol they reserve for the latter takes on a tone that could be mistaken, superficially, for anarchist. For example, Rothbard wrote, "Throughout history groups of men calling themselves 'the government' or 'the State' have attempted—usually successfully—to gain a compulsory monopoly of the commanding heights of the economy and the society. In particular, the State has arrogated to itself a compulsory monopoly over police and military services, the provision of law, judicial decision-making, the mint and the power to create money, unused land ("the public domain"), streets and highways, rivers and coastal waters, and the means of delivering mail." And again, "Taxation is theft, purely and simply, even though it is theft on a grand and colossal scale which no acknowledged criminals could hope to match. It is a compulsory seizure of the property of the State's inhabitants, or subjects."

For the libertarians, in a society without a state, freely undertaken contracts between individuals, equal before the law and remunerated according to the market, would serve to achieve their ideal.

Finally, it is worth nothing that anarcho-capitalists are state abolitionists and distinguish themselves from "minarchists" on this point. The latter advocate a state reduced to its sovereign functions, such as army, police, and justice—that is, functions strictly necessary for ensuring the security of persons and goods.

Anarcho-capitalists maintain that their position is authentically anarchist because they are antistate. They add that what distinguishes them from classical anarchists (or "leftists") is their belief that egalitarianism is an illusion. Failing to conceive of any form of equality besides legal equality, anarcho-capitalists assert that a free society will inevitably reflect real inequalities among individuals.

It is now time to say why these ideas are in no sense anarchist and why anarchists reject them.

While everyday language is often imprecise and inexact—which is why the sciences must often generate their own precise, unequivocal, and often mathematical terms—language used to speak about politics is particularly imprecise. It abounds with strange or contradictory concepts. In his novel *1984*, George Orwell invented "newspeak"; in which "slavery is freedom." Orwell's writing on this question is particularly illuminating, showing how degradation of language, accompanying and facilitating degradation of thought, serves propaganda. For example, the United States has a "Defense" Department, which spends most of its time attacking, most often poor and defenseless countries. Similarly, the Hitlerite regime and doctrine were called national socialism and, in Russia, the dictatorship called itself the Soviet Union, hijacking the beautiful word "soviet." Examples are not difficult to find. Anarcho-capitalists have invented several others: a defense of wage slavery and inequalities (even the most extreme); granting rights to private tyrannies called corporations (particularly transnationals), some aspects of which are taken more seriously than the rights of people; the refusal to take human rights into account; and rejecting solidarity and mutual aid. This is what is presented as anarchism in the newspeak of the anarcho-capitalists.

In fact, anarcho-capitalists commit a paralogism, a gross error of reason: in this instance, consisting of taking the part for the whole. Having correctly identified antistatism as a component of anarchism, they take it for all of anarchism and conclude that their position, also antistate, is therefore anarchist.

However, the antistatist position of anarchists is derived from a more fundamental position: the rejection of all illegitimate authority. From this clear starting point, anarchists have fought capitalism and the market economy consistently and without exception. This includes individualist anarchists, whom the anarcho-capitalists claim as their precursors. Consistent antiauthoritarians cannot subscribe to a capitalist concept of property any more than they can call for a market economy. They can only be disgusted by the power that usury and capital wield, and by workplaces where wage slavery flourishes. Anarcho-capitalists raise no objections to any of these things.

Nor are they greatly troubled by the resulting inequalities; they suggest that the worst excesses can be palliated by individual charity, if so wished. Acknowledging that they diverge from anarchists on this point, anarcho-capitalists assert that equality is impossible because we are all different. Anarchists are comfortable with this diversity, celebrating its richness of life. Their defense of equality goes beyond this truism, however. It is a defense of equity, which takes into account the circumstances of freedom. Without this, neither liberty nor freedom would mean a great deal. Refusing to take any of this into consideration, anarcho-capitalists accept all inequalities, including those that establish or perpetuate the most violent injustices.

This is exactly what Chomsky had in mind when, reviewing anarcho-capitalist positions, he said that they reflected "a doctrinal system which, if ever implemented, would lead to forms of tyranny and oppression that have few counterparts in human history." However, he added, "There isn't the slightest possibility that its (in my view, horrendous) ideas would be implemented, because they would quickly destroy any society that made this colossal error." Returning to the idea of "contracts" dear to the anarcho-capitalists, he concluded, "The idea of "free contract" between the potentate and his starving subject is a sick joke, perhaps worth some moments in an academic seminar exploring the consequences of (in my view, absurd) ideas, but nowhere else."

The concept of freedom promulgated by anarcho-capitalists is the cornerstone of its arguments. It couldn't be further from anarchist positions. The liberty of anarcho-capitalists is individual freedom, the freedom not to be obstructed. It is a negative freedom, conceived in a purely individualist way and upheld by a system of protection, which some wish to see privatized and which others recognize as state-dependent. This liberty, blind to the circumstances of its exercise, is extremely limited. Wage earners who are forced to sell themselves are said to be free. The freedom of anarcho-capitalists is that of the fox at liberty in a free-range henhouse. It's the freedom of gated communities in which the richest Americans escape from the chaos they've created. It's freedom chained to the slavery of others.

The anarcho-capitalist concept of freedom is so sterile that some anarcho-capitalists have even defended slavery, as the (provisional) freedom to alienate one's own freedom. This makes their doctrine unique in the history of modern—though not of all—political theory.

Remembering the clear anarchist rejection of the capitalist concept of property, and recalling the multitude of alternatives to this concept that anarchists have sought out and defended, there is no question that the anarcho-capitalist concept of property rights is unacceptable to anarchists. An exhaustive examination of this question would be long and technical. However, as Chomsky suggested in the following example, the anarcho-capitalist doctrine of rights and justice is already unacceptable to common sense. Let's suppose, Chomsky said, that through means that anarcho-capitalist theory accepts as legitimate, through luck and contracts "freely consented to" under pressure of need, one individual gains control over an element necessary to life. Everyone else would be forced either to sell themselves as slaves to this person (if he wants them) or perish. This is supposed to be a just society!

Anarcho-capitalists fail to understand or, at any rate, barely take into account the crucial role of the state in the genesis, development, and expansion of capitalism. Although they sometimes denounce the state that uses public funds to subsidize businesses, these supposed enemies of the state obviously remain silent about the state that guarantees the rights and privileges of these private tyrannies with the incredible power.

So what is left that can be considered truly anarchist? Opposition to the state? Even here, some anarchists are of the opinion, not without reason, that we live in a historical period in which the state must be provisionally defended and that this position does not constitute an intolerable distortion of anarchism. South American anarchists use a nice metaphor to explain their position on this issue. We are in a cage, they concede, in the cage of the state; but outside the cage lurks the lion of private tyrannies. For the moment, therefore, we content ourselves with expanding the size of the cage and refrain from breaking the bars.

CONCLUSION

This book is essentially about the events and ideas in the history of anarchism. In concluding, I would like to turn to the present and future, broaching certain questions that inevitably arise concerning the relevance and currency of these ideas, and their implications for us now. Many observers are in general agreement that there has been a revival of anarchism; many anarchists among them celebrate this fact. It seems true that anarchist history, practices, and theories have enjoyed a certain popularity in the past decade, if not longer. Similarly, I think it is fair to note that anarchism has inspired—to various degrees—movements, practices, and thought of all sorts, from the punk movement to the Zapatista uprising to some trends in feminism, ecologism, the animal rights movement, vegetarianism, and more. Yet even as I note this, I find it difficult to celebrate this renaissance without reserve.

The root of my hesitation is the following: the economic, political, and social order established at the planetary level since the beginning of the 1970s ("neoliberalism") is so oppressive for the majority of humans that alternatives such as those proposed by anarchism should be far better known and discussed than they are. There are no doubt many reasons for this deficit of knowledge, but I wish to focus on those that are, in my view, generally attributable to anarchists themselves. We can thus hope to discover avenues for reflection and action capable of deepening the influence of anarchism and its ideals in our era.

Most importantly: far too often, anarchists tend to pull back to positions that, in my view, constitute highly debatable or even deplorable choices. These contribute significantly to the misunderstanding of anarchist positions and help ensure that what is known is neither attractive nor mobilizing. In North America, this primarily takes the form of lifestyle activism, a term describing a wide variety of individual practices, in private life, which are presented as activism of the highest importance. This kind of activism is widespread today, particularly among anarchists who advocate and practice vegetarianism, ethical consumerism, primitivism, etc. These practices are often accompanied by their inverse: an attitude of condemnation of those who do not adhere to these practices or who carry out different practices. When vegetarianism is held up as a highly political practice, eating meat becomes a political error. Generalizing this type of analysis quickly leads to the condemnation of just about every aspect of our contemporaries' lifestyles: consumption, watching television, following professional sports, and so on. All of these activities, and many others, are deemed alienating and degrading, and refusing to participate in them is held to be a highly significant gesture.

This reality has its roots in the Keynesian period of Western bloc market economies. Keynesianism began at the end of the Second World War, with the Bretton Woods Agreement (1944).

For three decades, states played a preponderant role in the economy, notably by exercising tight control over the flow of capital and putting in place a series of measures (inspired by John Maynard Keynes) to stimulate demand. There ensued a net increase of productivity and growth as well as the establishment of a welfare state promoting social programs. Some anarchists reacted by concealing their opposition to the principle of the state, which they believed had become anachronistic, and advocated limiting action to small-scale, private-sphere projects, on the fringes of the large institutions. Colin Ward was among those who promoted this pragmatism, which blended contemporary forms of individualism with anarchist individualism of the past to form lifestyle activism. At base, this path leads to an impasse of theory and activism and is a mark and admission of impotence. It is a mistake to think that these practices have any real political bearing or to attribute them any great meaning or weight. Worse, those who adopt this stance sometimes cloak themselves in an isolating attitude of condescension, a mixture of purism and totally unjustifiable disdain, which, far from convincing those who encounter it, arouses disgust.

Moreover, another tendency glorifies a dark side of anarchism, isolating itself completely: under diverse guises and to various degrees, this current encourages a retreat into irrationalism—which anarchists have not always been able resist—and into violence. This tendency seems to be even more destructive when it is expressed as an intellectual posture of fatalism; the monotonal repetition that "everything is bad" with a refrain of proposals familiar to everyone, especially those whom anarchists should be engaging. This quickly degenerates into dogmatism: chanting slogans pulled from old theories and practices or sinking into prophecies of doom, all the more unattractive for often being ill-founded. The next step is to take refuge in purism; refusing all reformism and all struggles with immediate goals, even if these are compatible with the broader, long-term goals of anarchism.

The history of anarchism provides us with examples of activists and thinkers capable of much greater nuance and openness. It shows us that the richness and interest of anarchism has long resided in these virtues. It is high time to recall the principle of tolerance, of an "anarchism without qualification," that I cited at the beginning of this book. Applying this principle can provide the most valuable antidotes to the poisons of irrationalism and sectarism. Anarchists have for too long failed to advance credible proposals for social, economic, cultural, and political organization. It is primarily this lack of vision that prevents anarchism from once again inspiring the struggles and debates of our times. The work of Michael Albert and Robin Hahnel, whose model of participatory economy I outlined briefly earlier, seems to me to constitute a prime example of what is required. It is up to anarchists to put forward such alternatives—valuable for culture, politics, and society—and advance them in a nondogmatic way, in a spirit of tolerance, hope, and invitation to discussion. Anarchists did so in an era in which it was legitimate to claim that those they addressed had nothing to lose but their chains. This is no longer the case, and this type of work, carried out in the same spirit but seeking solutions to the questions and problems of today, is all the more necessary. The results could be valuable. First, such alternatives will help to respond to the objections inevitably leveled against anarchist positions. They will also help to clarify and articulate anarchist values in a more coherent way. Finally, and most importantly, they will allow achievable, short- or long-term goals to be set for activism.

It is impossible to say what the future holds for the outcome or role of anarchist theory. It nevertheless seems to me that this will depend, at least in part, on how anarchists carry out the work that I just outlined. The goal of these efforts and the values promoted by anarchism are well known. Noam Chomsky recently laid them out:

> The task for a modern industrial society is to achieve what is now technically realizable, namely, a society which is really based on free voluntary participation of people who produce and create, live their lives freely within institutions they control, and with limited hierarchical structures, possibly none at all.

Can this goal be achieved? Will it? I have no idea and I sincerely believe that we cannot answer such questions with any confidence.

However, I am persuaded that it is up to anarchists to convince people that this goal is still desirable and to maintain hope that it is reasonable to believe it can be attained.

Anarchism has been, and in my view must remain, a school of hope, rationality, and humanism.

Giving Chomsky the last word:

> I would like to believe that people have an instinct for freedom, that they really want to control their own affairs. They don't want to be pushed around, ordered, oppressed, etc., and they want a chance to do things that make sense, like constructive work in a way that they control or maybe control together with others. I don't know any way to prove this. It's really a hope about what human beings are like, a hope that if social structures change sufficiently, those aspects of human nature will be realized.

INDEX